New Perspectives on Liberal Education

New Perspectives on Liberal Education

Edited by Herbert Costner

University of Washington Press

Seattle and London

Library of Congress Cataloguing-in-Publication Data

New perspectives on liberal education / edited by Herbert Costner.
    p.   cm.
    ISBN 0-295-96679-3
    1. Education, Humanistic. 2. Education, Higher—1965–
  I. Costner, Herbert L., 1930–
  LC1011.N466 1988
  378—dc19   88-28201
                                                    CIP

Preface

It is a particular pleasure to be able to introduce this volume of articles, based on talks given to celebrate the University of Washington's one hundred and twenty-fifth anniversary.

During the past several years we have seen throughout the country and world an increased interest in, and criticism of, the ways we educate undergraduate students. Especially at large universities such as ours, it is claimed that there is no common curriculum for study, no focus among the vast array of courses that make up a degree program. Our College of Arts and Sciences, which locally bears the burden of these criticisms, decided to celebrate its anniversary by listening to new voices on an old theme; hence our title, "New Perspectives on Liberal Education."

Like other similar institutions, the University of Washington has made various changes, large and small, in its academic programs over the past several decades. Some wither away after a short time and are forgotten, and others flourish as acknowledged educational improvements. Several years ago, our faculty voted to establish a new, alternative general education program that will be offered be-

v

ginning in the fall of 1988. I have hopes that the College Studies Program will rank with the acknowledged improvements. It builds on what large universities are best prepared to do—combine the expansion of important disciplines of knowledge with education that challenges students to think for themselves. These efforts will no doubt continue. Thus, these talks have come at an opportune time.

There are many persons I want to thank for making this volume possible. The speakers in the series were gracious in accepting our invitaton, and they rose to the challenge posed by the topic. I am grateful to Professors Herb Costner, Constantine Christofides, Donna Gerstenberger, Ronald Geballe, and Solomon Katz for their assistance in conceiving and organizing the series. I thank President William P. Gerberding and Dean Gene Woodruff of the Graduate School, as well as television station KING 5 and the law firm of Foster, Pepper & Riviera, for their financial support. Above all, I thank Jean Leed for her assistance from the beginning. She, more than anyone, made it possible for the occasion to be both a celebration and a challenging intellectual event.

ERNEST M. HENLEY
Professor of Physics and former Dean
of the College of Arts and Sciences,
University of Washington

A Mind Lively and at Ease

ROGER SALE

3

Liberal Education
in a Post-Modern World

ELIZABETH KENNAN

25

Defining Our Future:
The Liberal Arts in Contemporary Society

RICHARD W. LYMAN

41

One Culture
The True Liberalism

DENYS WILKINSON

61

New Perspectives on Liberal Education

A Mind Lively and at Ease

ROGER SALE

WHEN THE UNIVERSITY OF WASHINGTON OPENED ITS doors in 1861, it was not a university, it was not a college, it was barely a high school. Since the territory was only six years old, and Seattle was ten, and the oldest white settlement was less than fifty, it is not surprising that formal education, especially higher education, was not much on anyone's mind or within anyone's grasp. It was almost twenty years before this university granted its first bachelor's degree. But, struggling and unformed though the university was in those years, its mold was being cast, not here, but farther east. The Morrill Act of 1862 established the framework for the great land grant public universities, especially in the western two-thirds of the country where the older, church-oriented colleges had not become a fixture; Illinois was founded in 1867, Ohio State in 1870, in conditions more affluent and more immediately aspiring than anything in Seattle; in 1869 Ezra Cornell said he would found an institution in which any person could find instruction in any subject; a year later, Charles W. Eliot, the founder of the elective system, became president of Harvard; Johns Hopkins, with an enormous initial endow-

3

ment, began in 1876. This university's mold was being cast because from its first breath it has wanted to be what those others were then becoming; what they valued, it has valued.

The modern American university emerged in the embrace of two related principles: first, its teachers should be experts in specifically named fields of study, and, second, anything that could be made into an academic study had a proper place on the campus, with a status roughly equal to that of any other. These principles were then buttressed and shaped by importations from European universities; if Washington were to grow up imitating Michigan, so Michigan grew up imitating Leipzig and Berlin. From Europe came the department, the laboratory, the seminar, the library, and the rapidly burgeoning social sciences. Via the land grant university came programs in agriculture, veterinary medicine, mining, forestry, fisheries, and education. So by the time our university granted its first degree, what it would do, and how it would do it, had been established for it, mostly in the years since its founding.

Perhaps because it all seems so obvious now, it also seems inevitable: this is life, this is industrial democracy, this is the sun rising in the east. It may thus seem inevitable that certain words to describe university faculty members became honorific: along with *expert, professional, distinguished, eminent, internationally famous, prize-winning;* concerning what is preferable—*advanced, published* and *publishable, specialty, specialized,* and, even better, *highly specialized;* which left little doubt what to make of *elementary* and *beginner, amateur* and *amateurish, dilletante, crank, populist, popular, parochial,* and *provincial.* It may also seem inevitable that the people who earned the honored titles became the most highly paid and, by a paradox peculiar to the academic world, the ones who taught the fewest courses and the fewest students. It may seem inevitable that those branches of the university which command the highest value in the market place—medicine, engineering, law—became the most respected and highly rewarded branches within the university.

Given many strong historical forces at work in the last century and a half, we can say that all this *was* inevitable. But, if only to suggest what might at least qualify as a rejected alternative, I quote from the beginning of Title Seven of the constitution of the state of Washington: "It is the paramount duty of the state to educate its children." When the constitution was written, there were fewer than three hundred college level students at the University of Washington, so the term "children" may not seem surprising. Since 1889, though, the state has expanded "children" to include all those enrolled in the various community colleges and state universities; for these the state provides most of the financial support. Effectively, what the constitution designates as "children," the state has since understood as "citizens."

Was it inevitable that the state should understand "to educate," when schools of higher education were in question, in terms inherited by the University of Washington from the universities of Michigan, Illinois, Wisconsin, and the like? Yes, it is hard to think otherwise now. If the citizens of Michigan, Illinois, and Wisconsin acquiesced to their universities in this matter—give us your distinguished, your expensive, your internationally famous—why should the citizens of Washington, or their representatives, think differently? Each state that could afford one wanted "a great research university," though no one seems to have asked very hard about the relation between that desire and the paramount duty of the state to educate its citizens. My question begins here: since the university, like any institution, seeks to be self-perpetuating on its own terms, can we, you and I, thinking of ourselves as citizens as well as members of the university community, imagine the verb "to educate" differently from the way large American universities have done for a century and more? Do we have to think that graduate education, and specialization, and "scholarship" and the rest are the *heart* of the matter?

I come at the question of liberal education this way for a number of reasons. First, to assert that liberal education is a stranger and an alien on a campus like this one—not unknown, sometimes tolerated and even admired, little sought and frequently shunned. It is only by asserting this that it seems fruitful to raise the question of liberal education at all. Second, while I cannot truly claim to offer a new perspective on liberal education, I very much want to avoid some of the old perspectives, which are irrelevant here anyway. In some of the old debates about liberal education it was frequently asked if some knowledge were more worth knowing than other knowledge; what was to happen to the old fixed curriculum of classical education in liberal arts colleges or liberal arts components of universities? I suspect that privately many of us feel that knowing this is indeed more important than knowing that, but we are content to keep our feelings private. It is bad enough that the academic reward systems express as well as echo the market values of the society at large; I need not vent my feeling about that state of affairs by installing myself as the philosopher king and telling you that what I know is more important than what you know. Third, if I focus on the education of the citizenry I avoid the ancient assumption that some people are more worth educating than others, and its corollary, that education for all ends up as education for none. In this setting, and on this occasion, it is important to say that while we cannot educate all, we can try. We can regret that we cannot educate all, even as we acknowledge that liberal education is not something anyone can offer, like test scores and diplomas, on a mass scale.

So, for my purposes, any subject is as good as another, and at least in principle, any learner is as good as another. In asking you to think about liberal education, I would like you to think about education as liberation, as freeing, and to ask how the paramount duty of the state might be to seek such liberating—minds lively and at ease.

My title comes from Jane Austen's *Emma*. It concerns what a young woman sees and thinks while standing at the door of a shop in an English village a hundred and seventy-five years ago. That context is sufficiently different from our own that I need to say why I want it. If asked to say what a university seeks as its goal, most people would quickly answer: knowledge. I want to suggest that in a university, it is often knowledge that enslaves, not ignorance. Emma Woodhouse, the young woman in question, has little knowledge. Though she is fond of drawing up lists of books she might read, she has never finished a book in her life. Still, I want to take this moment of hers in front of the shop as a model for a liberated mind.

Emma begins enslaved indeed, and ignorant. She has never been outside her village; she has never done more than dabble at anything she has been asked to learn. This, though, is only a symptom of her difficulty. She is clever, handsome, and rich, the princess of her village—and she is bored. She enslaves herself with fantasy, not of the Emma Bovary, daydreaming kind, but of the intellectually lazy kind that lets her imagine that what she wants to see is what is really there. She connives at the love lives of others; she tries to arrange marriages.

Slowly, and often painfully, Emma comes to see the prison in which she has placed herself. The passage I want to examine comes when Emma is well along in her education, though, like most of us, she is better at seeing objects in the middle distance than those close to her. In this incident, nothing close to her is pressing in. She and a friend have gone to the store; the friend is dithering over her purchases, so Emma goes "to the door for amusement":

> Much could not be hoped from the traffic of even the busiest part of Highbury;—Mr. Parry walking hastily by; Mr. William Cox letting himself in at the office-door, Mr. Cole's carriage horses returning from exercise; or a stray letter-boy on an obstinate mule, were the liveliest objects she could presume to expect; and when her eyes fell only on the butcher with his tray, a tidy old woman travelling homewards from shop with her full basket, two curs quarrelling over a dirty bone, and a string of dawdling children round the baker's little bow-window eyeing the ginger bread, she knew she had no reason to complain, and was amused enough; quite enough still to stand at the door. A mind lively and at ease can do with seeing nothing, and can see nothing that does not answer. (Chap. 27)

Emma's first perception is offered within the frame of "much could not be hoped" and "her eyes fell only." By beginning with "much could not be hoped," Austen seems to tease Emma: she could not hope to see much; she is a famous snob; she looks only for food for her fantasies. Yet in the two lists that follow, one naming the most that could be hoped for, the other saying what she actually sees, we recognize that no one could hope for *much* here.

Like everyone else, Emma cannot be expected to find

constant interest in things that are and will remain at some distance, but if she can find no interest at all in what she sees, she is in trouble. Emma's world is small, but she lives in it and must learn to do so without the false stimulant of fantasy. Seeing the butcher, the old woman, the quarreling dogs, and the children, "she knew she had no reason to complain"; she had come to the door of the shop for amusement, and now she cannot complain when what she sees is not fascinating. She "was amused enough." It is a small moment, but the real test of how and how well we are educated can be judged by our response in such small moments. Austen has reason to want to claim something large for it: "A mind lively and at ease can do with seeing nothing, and can see nothing that does not answer." There is "nothing" in this scene facing Emma, and each item taken by itself is unremarkable. Yet because Emma's lively mind is for once at ease, she moves past the snobbery of "much could not be hoped," past "seeing nothing," and comes to rest in seeing "nothing that does not answer."

Emma's mind is herein free, liberated, disinterested. She has things yet to learn and mistakes to make, but insofar as she can do with seeing nothing, and can see nothing that does not answer, she has achieved, in miniature, the goal of liberal education. I cannot define such a mind, but I can say this much about it: it knows what it knows in a way that enables it to take the next moment, the next object that is put before it, and to be receptive, alert for mystery or confusion or inability, but quick to establish relations between what it knows and the next moment, the new thing, the what happens next. What Emma can hope for in the street scene is not much, and perhaps what she sees is even less than that much; but she sees, she adjusts, she comes for amusement and is amused enough. In the liberated mind, knowledge is all verbs: I see, I don't see, I haven't yet seen, I understand.

Now let us come back to the university setting and ask what happens here that inhibits or prohibits liberal education much of the time. You will not have missed my tone when I touched earlier upon words like *expert, distinguished, specialty,* and *specialized.* I am myself quite happy to be an expert on some matters literary and historical, and I often enjoy the feeling of a conversation with a colleague, another expert, on such matters. But there are terrible limitations to knowledge conceived as matters of expertise and specialty, and most people in universities seem unaware or oblivious of them. If I am an expert, and if I assume that the important fact about my knowledge is that I am indeed an expert, my way of speaking to you, who are not an expert but a beginner, a student, is always going to be along the lines of: "I have what you want. Here is what I know and you should learn, and can I be of any help?" Expert knowledge is mostly nouns—things possessed, handed over, or passed on. In expert knowledge we speak of adding to the sum of what is known, and of someone's making a contribution to knowledge, as though it were a treasure hoard.

The obvious sin of knowledge thus conceived is pride, the tendency that then becomes a habit that conveys this sense: "On this safe ground of my expertise I *know,* and you know less, and since I can tell beginner from intermediate from advanced, I can tell precisely how much less you know than I." But, as with most pride, the underlying sin is despair, self-pity, giving up, because even as the expert says, "I know," the other message is: "I can know this but I cannot know that, or not in the same way." To be sure, if we take two unrelated subjects, like medieval literature and low temperature physics, then the expert in one is always going to be saying about the other, "I can't know that, or not in the same way." But when the person who is "in" medieval literature, conceiving of knowledge as specialty, says to the person in Victorian or American literature, "I must defer to you about this candidate, or that article, or this text, because I don't know enough to judge it," then pride of knowledge has in effect become self-pity and despair. "There is just too much to know," says the expert. "I can know only a tiny bit of it." Thus it is that in a university it is often knowledge that enslaves; when one is paralyzed by "all there is to know," one is thinking of *knowing* only as a matter of knowing expertly. Such paralysis may drive one to more expert knowledge, but it will not lead to freedom.

Most of us, George Eliot says in a context only partially different, walk around well wadded with stupidity. What begins whenever a teacher says, "I know, and you don't, and that is the crucial difference between us," is stupidity. My mind enslaves your mind, and your mind can then neither make itself free nor be freed by anything my mind does. The best you can hope to do is, like Good King Wenceslas's page, follow in the master's footsteps and arrive at where I already am. The subject is *Emma,* conceived not by minds lively and at ease, but by Austen scholars. They are approached by an aspiring Austen scholar, to whom the message they offer is as follows: "Maybe you have something original to say about *Emma,* and maybe you don't. In order to find out, read what others have written about this novel, and, by seeing what they have said, you will discover what has not been written before." I doubt if anyone puts it that crudely; no one would dare. But it is how expert teacher implicitly speaks to aspiring student when knowledge is conceived as a dragon's treasure hoard, and it is a stupid statement that leads to stupid writing about *Emma.*

If the alternative to this involves seeing knowledge not as nouns but verbs, then we need not so much ask after the attributes of the liberated mind as try to describe what different relation of teacher to student might be involved. We can start by saying that because it is the liberation of the mind of the student that is essential, the mind of the teacher is less important as the focal point of the action than the mind of the student. And the moment we say that what the student knows, and how the student knows it, is crucial, we have run into the matter of discipline, perhaps without knowing it. The aim of liberal education is discipline, conceived not as a noun or a subject, but as a verb, an act of mind. The difference here between noun and verb is the difference between discipline, which essentially seeks freedom, and obedience, which essentially seeks enslavement. Put that way, the difference between the two seems obvious, but the difference can easily be confounded, as can be seen when we remember that one definition of discipline involves punishment and obedience.

Discipline conceived as a liberating activity creates ways of making knowledge active, so that when the new moment happens, the new object comes into view, relations can be established, places of confusion or ignorance can be identified, and the new thing can be placed in a context of the already known. Knowledge conceived as a matter of expertise tends to be clumsy, so that the expert can look at the new thing and either accept it as being part of the field of knowledge, the treasure hoard, or else spit it out, rejected, as not germane or not acceptable because not expert. Knowledge conceived as a verb, an action between teacher and student, seeks situations where discipline must be sought by the student, where mess and confusion are acknowledged and their elimination is hoped for, where the student must flounder to discover whatever discipline is available to relate the new and the old, the strange and the familiar. But if discipline is to liberate, it must be a verb, an act the student performs, and so it is not something the teacher can know, it is not something the teacher can impart, or pass on, to the student.

Students have been known to say: "That teacher made us think." Strictly speaking, this is impossible, since no one can force another to think. But if we ask what might be involved that can lead to this conclusion, we can imagine a teacher who offers no lecture notes, no how-to-do-it demonstrations, no statement of what is wanted. All the time the teacher is putting new things in front of the students, or new ways to see familiar things, or forgotten ways of feeling and knowing. If the teacher then leaves the students alone to make what they can of the new thing, the teacher can then respond to what the students do. The teacher is always urging, questioning, condemning, always trying to indicate that the goal is not to know more or to be more expert, except incidentally, but to know so the knower is smarter, more alert, less stupid, more able.

The role of the teacher's knowledge in all this can never be a fixed matter, since when it becomes fixed it changes from a verb to a noun, which is why almost all that goes under the name of testing and examinations is self-pitying, self-deluding, Emma's narcotic of fantasy turned into a fantasy about knowing. The teacher must always be gauging and guessing, about the nature of the ignorance the teacher is facing, right now; how much simple explaining or narrating is needed before the floundering of the students can be assumed not to lead to drowning. Expertise is often a positive hindrance here. The expert can often find it hard to comprehend or tolerate the ignorance or the inertness of the inexpert student; the expert can be tempted into wishing that the undergraduates would be more like graduates, and the graduates more like those colleagues who qualify as fellow experts. The experts often become trapped in the wish, or the insistence, that their knowledge becomes my knowledge, or else, no count.

The model of liberal education is dialogue, conversation made more intent than our usual ones by the artifice of class hours, deadlines, papers, comments on the same. It may not be conversation among equals, but it is conversation where what one person thinks is every bit as important as what anyone else thinks. The success of the teacher depends almost entirely on the ability of the teacher to convey to the students that they are responsible for their own education, and, therefore, for their parts of the conversation. The ball must go back into the students' court as often as possible, because the more the teacher keeps the ball, examines it, explains it, the more encouraged the students are to become passive and obedient, and to think that what they should be doing is the best imitation of the teacher they can manage. Such minds are neither lively nor at ease. It is easier, to be sure, if the teacher keeps the ball—easier for both teacher and student. The short term progress that can be made working this way often makes it seem preferable to the more confusing, more unsettling, less organized conversations that are the heart of the matter that seeks the freeing of minds. Of course, there are plenty of occasions for straightforward examining and explaining, but the best occasions for these come when the students ask the questions that describe or reveal their knowledge, their ignorance, their confusion. At this point the students have named their stake in the matter, and the teacher is less likely to carry coals to Newcastle, or to explain something the students have little chance of understanding.

It is not always easy to find ways to convey: "It is not what is on my mind, but what is on yours, that counts most here." It is especially difficult in something like a lecture course, where passive, obedient learning seems built right into the process. But, regardless of the format, I think the first step in conveying this message is to acknowledge that part of the mystery of learning is that it happens not by moving from order to order, but from mess and confusion to order. Any expert might grant that mess and confusion are necessary evils in teaching; I would rather say that mess and confusion must be created, must be embraced even, as the breeding ground from which order, clarity, and discipline will come.

Whenever I talk to teachers of composition, I invariably run into resistance the moment I try to say just that. In that context, it will usually take the form of my saying: "You give the student the assignment, and you comment on what the student writes, but in between, the whole messy business of writing a paper, that is the student's territory and the teacher must keep out." "But," comes the anguished reply, "if I don't help them, they won't see how to organize their essays," or, "At least I need to give them some options." But to do that is just like persistently interrupting the other person in a conversation, or, worse, like turning writing a paper into an obedience test. One is trying to pay respect to the minds of the students, one is trying to have the students respect their own minds. If they know that the teacher is paying careful attention, that is all the presence the students need; the rest is theirs, their confusion, their mess, their clarity, their discipline, and if not theirs, no count.

One result of this is that the teacher cannot anticipate very much, and the clarity of the teacher may not have more than a family resemblance to the clarity of a student struggling to become free. Not long ago a colleague of mine met someone who had been a student in classes of mine years ago, and the former student, now an excellent professor of genetics here, said that what he had learned from my classes was the importance of a sense of fact. Granted that one must take this as the residue from experiences of twenty-five years ago, but still, I was puzzled when I heard this because I don't think I have ever in my life spoken about the importance of a sense of fact, though I know it is often crucial. So the student had read some old poems, and I had offered some commentary on them, some history for a context, perhaps, and I'm sure I had conveyed the insistence that he damned well had to learn *something*. But what I "taught," in one sense, is not what he "learned," and yet I am quite sure we were both tending to business as best we could, and neither of us, of course, need be dismayed at the outcome.

I cannot now tell you, alas, what the moment-to-moment conversation was between me and the student back then, but I can, actually, go back many years before that to one of the great learning events of my own life, and I hope the example will not seem trivial because it is simple and happened to a seven year old. In this case the teacher did nothing more than insist by her patient silence that I must try. We were reading a book, and on one page was a picture of a cow, and on the next page was a picture of a different cow, and this sentence: "Here is another cow." I was astonished when I found myself seeing two words, "an" and "other," which I had seen, inside this third word, which I also knew but had never seen. It was as though I were making up the language myself, and the mystery and power of that moment is shiningly clear to me almost half a century later. The teacher could have told me it was "an other," and she could have shown me dozens of words that were made from combining two other words. She could have been, thereby, an expert. Instead, and I am sure with no clue as to the success of what she was doing, she waited, admitted the mess, and created the possibility for a clarifying discipline. And part of the mystery of learning is that I, of course, have no clue as to why this moment, and not the many others when a teacher asked and patiently waited while I floundered and nothing whatsoever happened, was the moment of clarifying discipline. And, I hope, this story conveys a sense of why most discussion of "teaching methods" is folly. The teacher is seldom sure when to be active or when to be passive in the dialogue.

I have, by this last anecdote, brought us back closer to the matter of the citizenry of the state of Washington. One reason, perhaps, my story of myself in the second grade doesn't seem like much is that people tend to agree that in the education of most people, in the early school years, knowledge is almost all verbs—learning to read, write, and work with numbers—and most people agree that it is usually very exciting to have moments like mine with "another," where it is clear how discipline can lead to freedom. But school gets grayer for most after a few years, and shades of the prison house begin to fall. One way of saying why this happens is that knowledge gets shifted from verbs to nouns, from knowing how to knowing what, and the hows become, increasingly, a "Let me show you."

Yet I do not think this needs to happen. If it were understood that all classes went on being what they were in the first years—namely, introductions to reading and writing and working with numbers—then one could teach any subject with the teachers and students always on the frontier, the students being asked to look at what they do not know, the teachers groping for what to say that will be of greatest help, and when to say it. This would be more easily accomplished if we didn't have English teachers, history teachers, biology teachers, and the like, but just teachers, each trying to demonstrate the qualities of a liberated mind by looking for ways to teach a variety of subjects. A mind lively and at ease can move onto the frontier more readily and more enablingly than the mind that stresses obedience, ignorance, and expertise, since the latter mind is so easily convinced that it cannot do anything much with a subject it does not know expertly.

But to do all this is hard work, and it cannot be done by teachers and students working under the conditions currently endured in the public schools; if real learning takes place where students daily take five or six subjects, and teachers daily face five or six groups of students, it must be counted a miracle. Normally I teach two hours a day, and I know I can manage three, but that is the maximum. It should be the maximum in all schools at all levels. The ideal school day might proceed like this: begin with the exhausting mental work, in maybe three segments of forty-five minutes each, from nine until noon. Then break for a leisurely lunch. Then bring on the coaches, the music and the drama people, because discipline of the body, the hands, the voice is important, almost as important as that of the mind during many of these years. The beautiful fact about both body and mind is that discipline can make each, however strenuous the work, lively and at ease, and the energies expended in gaining the discipline can thereby be self-renewing.

Why should we think of college and university life as anything more than a continuation of this process? Why not continue to say that what we are doing is learning to read, write, and work with numbers? As minds grow they can do larger tasks, of course, and the experience of living almost always can be made to help the experience of school, of intellectual life. But I do not exaggerate when I say that the key task for the director of a doctoral dissertation is that of teaching composition, doing essentially the things that the fourth-grade teacher does when teaching writing. The doctoral candidate knows much more and has a longer attention span, so he or she can be expected to be more consecutive along a much longer line of thought than the nine year old, but writing is writing, making words where no words were.

In all this I hope I have not implied that there is no place for experts and expertise. There is nothing wrong with knowing something thoroughly, or with scholarly projects that take years to complete; what's wrong is to have this aspect of learning enshrined as the heart and soul of university life, and there is no better perspective from which to see this than that of thinking about the education of the citizenry. My sense is that only the liberated mind can truly know the value of expertise, just as only the liberated mind can stand on a street corner, see nothing, and see nothing that does not answer. My sense also is that some people are always going to enjoy becoming experts, and that when, as an adolescent stumbling through school, I became an expert on both baseball and American popular music from 1920 to 1945, what I lacked is what Frank Morgan tells Ray Bolger he lacks in *The Wizard of Oz*—not brains but a diploma. If our universities were focusing on the liberating of minds, we could, in effect, sneak up on the matter of expertise, watch some people become experts just because they chose to, and then say to them, after they had worked awhile in some corner of the vineyard: "What you now need is a plaque pronouncing you expert." Universities are excellent places for people to become expert in odd things, too, in knowledges difficult to acquire, but it is implausible to have this kind of expertise stand as the aim of formal public education.

What does the citizenry need? The task may be the simple but very elusive one of living decently and well; it may be that of listening to music, watching a movie or a ballet, with intelligent pleasure; it may be that of striving for an intelligent, or even an intelligible, body politic; it may be that of exploring what currently are the frontiers of medicine or philosophy. In every case, the mind one wants is free, nimble, lively, at ease. Further, it has long been known how easy and foolish it is to train people for work that is liable to become obsolete shortly after the training is completed; in most businesses and professions what is wanted is not so much expert knowledge as the capacity to relate the new thing to the already known in an active and inquiring way.

Yet, for all that, what are the chances for the pursuit of liberal education on a campus like this one? In one sense, not bad at all. No one has ever stopped a teacher here from trying to engage with students in a way that will help free their minds. But remember this: the most frequently used word for teaching in most parts of the university is "instruct," and "instruct" means "to furnish with knowledge, especially by a systematic method," "to furnish with information," "to direct or command." We all know what *that* means, and no instructor seeks minds lively and at ease among the instructed. It also means that students who are geared towards the expert, the professional, the school that will lead directly to a job, and who have been geared that way for most of their lives, can be quickly bewildered, and soon angered, when asked to engage in a different relation with what they know. It isn't that such students seek to be faceless technocrats in what some like to call an increasingly complex society; it is only that they have learned to have their minds furnished with knowledge, especially by a systematic method; they have learned habits of passivity and enslavement, so of course they may protest when these are not only not called for but are implicitly repudiated.

In case remembering this about university teaching being given over to instruction is not enough to make one gloomy about the prospects for liberal education here, let me descend briefly to the realm of the mercenary. A couple of months ago I came into class and was asked if I'd seen the list in the *Daily* of the university's hundred most highly paid faculty members. No. Why, I was asked, was I not on the list? Naively, I answered that I probably wasn't among the second one hundred either. When I saw the list myself, I realized I might well not be among the first thousand; and I am the author of lots of books, *published* books, and I am considered sufficiently *distinguished* and *eminent* that I have been asked to speak to you tonight. No institution that pays, or pays off, according to a scale of value that treasures the expert, especially the expert whose knowledge is so highly specialized as to be all but unintelligible to more than half a dozen people in the state, is an institution that is about to turn itself around and say to the citizenry of the state: "Come, where it is not our expertise but our willingness always to start over that we value most about ourselves, and will value most in you." Nor does the fact that, among the most highly paid members of the faculty, only one teaches in the College of Arts and Sciences make me believe that matters are different here; the system of reward is essentially the same, only it works on a lower scale.

But I love teaching here, for reasons that have nothing to do with the university's stance towards itself, its teachers, its students. I have learned about myself that I would rather teach here than somewhere else where an idea of liberal education is affirmed. One reason is that here one can entertain the dream that the paramount duty of the state is to educate its citizens. But "citizens" is really a term best suited for speeches. It is not one that I, at least, walk around using. As to one of the ones I do use. . . .

After Dean Henley called me last fall and asked me to be part of this series, I felt honored to be asked, to be sure. But for reasons I probably have made clear, I also felt uneasy. Me? If they really want me, have I perhaps misrepresented myself all this while? Later that morning I walked across the quadrangle towards my class and I felt, suddenly and strongly, a feeling that I was at a loss to explain. It was love, clearly, love for all these people, these strangers, who were on the quadrangle with me. It was a number of days before I could see from where the feeling had come. The idea of speaking here tonight had made me uncomfortable, but then, walking to class, I had felt not just comfortable but positively at home with these hundreds of strangers.

Because the nearer I get to the classroom, the more likely it is that I will see someone, a stranger before the term began, but now a fellow laborer for these ten weeks, at this hour, with these books. More likely than not, the person will leave my life when the term is over, but, at least this is the hope, we will never quite be strangers to each other again. We will not have become more advanced, but, and again this is the hope, we will have become more free, more able to face the next book, the next stranger. Names, and titles of books, nouns, have been turned into verbs. It feels a sacred trust, a pact one makes with oneself, and with the most faceless stranger in the back of the class.

Liberal Education
in a Post-Modern World

Elizabeth T. Kennan

LIBERAL EDUCATION, THE SUBJECT OF UNRESOLVED
debate for at least the one hundred twenty-five years of this
distinguished university's life, is again a matter of our
urgent concern. Under attack in the press as inefficient, and
subject to doubt in the minds of students as irrelevant, the
"liberal arts" are nonetheless the architectural forms by
which we erect our ideal of higher education in America.
Because we believe that some principles underlie our designs, that some truths may be transmitted through them,
we can be passionate in our discussions.

Quietly as it began, the debate that first reached the national press from Harvard in 1977 posed the question of
academic architectonics and raised our tempers once again.
It presented the possibility, although never the actuality, of
a core program for the first two years of college. Challenged
from Cambridge, we were made to wonder whether a form
of education called "liberal," created in eighteenth century
New England and based then upon a single body of metaphysical and moral texts, could serve a purpose at this turn
into the twenty-first century. If it could, how could we
grasp and how articulate that form?

As universities have contemplated the possibilities of a new formalism in curriculum, their faculties might well feel a *frisson* of recognition in the urban landscapes they inhabit. Everywhere we look, the society is newly preoccupied with form. After two generations that stripped our public buildings and our private spaces of lines that either decorate or harmonize, our architects have once again discovered Chippendale. Patterns of elegant eighteenth century dining have offered designs for rooftop finials on Madison Avenue, and on this coast, classical overlays in strong color decorate the Portland Building some miles to the south. A feast of formalism meets the investor's eye among the new buildings of Austin, Texas, and Philip Johnson is even now laying a post modern footprint in Boston's Back Bay.

Both architects and their critics have recently turned upon midcentury modernism for its geometrical and abstract shapes, outlined in minimal fashion by glass and steel. They have rejected the intellectual hauteur that stripped these buildings of their contexts, both historical and actual, and they have questioned the mighty premise, best stated by Le Corbusier, that society itself could be cleansed by the purity of its architecture. The aching dullness of our urban landscapes has been commentary enough on the reproduction of styles taken from the Seagram or Lever Buildings, while the heartbreaking proliferation of vandalism and self-violence in vast modernist housing projects has given the lie to any transfer from the order of geometry to the order of life. Indeed, Charles Jencks, the English historian of architecture, dates the death of modern architecture with the destruction of the Pruitt-Igoe housing project in Saint Louis in 1972,[1] a project that had been honored by the American Institute of Architecture some twenty years before and that had embodied all the theorems of urban and architectural minimalism.

Educational programs in this country—like architectural ones—have known their own minimalism and are also playing once again with form. Indeed, we detonated our dynamite among the structures of postwar curricula even before the Pruitt-Igoe project went down in 1972. Very few of the lines and almost none of the decoration of general education survived the student agitation of the 1960s, and our own attempts in the past decade to revive form in the curricula have all been to some extent historicist.

Articulated in a New England Protestant environment, the assumption of liberal education was the belief in continuity between the formative texts of Christianity and the secular purposes of free men in a new republic. That secular purpose was caught most trenchantly in the early nineteenth century by Horace Mann, who argued for a more strictly democratic, that is to say political, education to modify the religious purposes that had informed college curricula up to that moment. As he wrote in the 1830s, the nation was undergoing violent change: rapid expansion and enormous growth by immigration of populations diverse in language and political traditions. Mann's purpose was to create a new unity based on common knowledge of political and moral texts which could encircle an area of agreement, or at least of compromise, in which free men could enact their public lives. A liberal education in the mid-nineteenth century clearly did not create a general will, but it did circumscribe the debate about values, even in a theater of war.

Prescribed college education did not long survive the Civil War. Mann's program of common study was attacked and almost entirely defeated in the late century by Harvard's towering President Charles Eliot, whose determination to introduce the specialization so fruitful in European universities swept away the old political agreements about higher education and, indeed, went a long way to replace colleges with universities. The force of Eliot's victory was such that he pulled all of higher education towards a departmental curriculum made of a plethora of specialities. From the beginning, the student was at liberty to choose. Convinced that education could best be conducted in courses and in seminars that led to research and that honed skills for the acquisition, or better yet, the discovery of knowledge, most faculties expended their efforts to build the research capacities of their classrooms.

When correction to this trend was suggested, it was a correction of degree only. Again at Harvard, after the turn of the century, President Abbott Lowell raised the question of the result of such specialization for the individual student and called for some mechanism that would ensure breadth as well as intensiveness of instruction. The debate turned upon a distribution of courses in the first two years of college, and the call was for students to become acquainted with more than one field. In most places the debate did not touch the premises of specialized education, but turned on questions of how many fields of knowledge a student should encounter in four years. Should there be only one field of study? Or, in an echo of an earlier Christian world, should there be a Trinity—an introduction to natural science, social science, and humanities? Most university and college faculties hovered about these niceties of number while a few daring educators in a few institutions willing to accept risk experimented with the older form, with the transmission of a body of texts intimate to the formation of the democratic ethos. The University of Wisconsin with the leadership of Alexander Meiklejohn, the University of Chicago, and St. John's College in Annapolis articulated and embodied a classicism based upon great inherited texts which was (and, at St. John's, still is) both formal and gracious, both rigorous and humane. But these experiments, though they offered an important counterpoise to the weight of opinion about American higher education, did not shift it before the 1940s. The crucial change was accomplished only by the shock of the Second World War, and that shock was articulated first at Eliot's own university. In 1943 President James Bryant Conant convened the Harvard faculty to consider the state of education in the nation. The result two years later was the famous Redbook entitled, *General Education in a Free Society*. Pressed by the revelations of war, Conant contended:

> The heart of the problem of a general education is the continuance of the liberal and humane tradition. Neither the mere acquisition of information nor the development of special skills and talents can give the broad basis of understanding which is essential if our civilization is to be preserved.[2]

Like Horace Mann a century earlier, Conant and his committee were searching for a theory of general education which would encompass change but would also create unity for the enactment of public life. The faculty realized that, in its originating form, American agreement about public life was religious, but with a certain explicit sadness, they put that aside as impractical in the modern world. What they would not put aside was the "impulse to mold students to a pattern sanctioned by the past." If this were ever to be absent from education, argued the committee, "*society would become discontinuous*" (italics mine).[3]

Even so, the Harvard faculty did not adopt a single body of texts to create continuity for every undergraduate. Instead, they profoundly revised the notion of "distribution." The simple introduction to different fields and methods of knowledge was to be replaced with study of a tightly defined body of materials. In the humanities, each student would study a choice of texts from our inherited high culture, drawing on the Bible, Plato, Dante, Shakespeare, Milton, Tolstoy, and, presumably, others.[4] In the social sciences, students would share a course examining the institutional and theoretical aspects of society.[5] And in the sciences, any introductory course would be created to convey the interrelationships, the history, and the methods of science, so that the rigor of experimental testing and its claims to veracity would be shared by all.[6] Unity, however, was not to be found in a combination of these courses or even of three, more senior and more specialized courses, taken later to complement them. It was to be found in the manner of teaching and learning, in its architectonic style:

> It is clearly of much more importance that honest thinking, clearness of expression and the habit of gathering and weighing evidence before forming a conclusion be encouraged than it is that students be required to take any particular group of introductory courses.[7]

The presumption of the Harvard faculty in 1945 was that the shared mode of our civilization to be conveyed to the young was once again its *belief*, this time its belief in reason. There was an assurance that reason, methodically experienced, could produce truth, and that all who were party to the transaction would recognize that truth if not as prescriptive, then certainly as persuasive. This in itself would clear the arena for productive and peaceful political action.

The postwar curriculum was not solely political. The great texts and the sequential semester in art or literature which would complete the preliminary course were not presented only as guideposts to reason. The Redbook recognized that human dignity, not simply human necessity, is the aim for a free society. Within that dignity lies depth of the spirit and diversion of wit as well as the determination of reason. The new concept of distribution was to include all three, not merely to broaden the mind, but to animate it. In the decade after 1945, most universities and colleges in the country adopted some form of the core curriculum the Redbook had pleaded for. In many, the notion of a preliminary selection of classical western texts to be read under a humanities rubric was replaced by an "introduction to western civilization," usually located in history departments. Programs in social science often replaced the study of "institutional and theoretical structures" with introductions to politics or to economics. But in the natural sciences, the notions of empirical methods, their tests for accuracy and then for veracity, remained constant, and with them went an intended respect for reason in its most palpable form.

We all know now that this renaissance of form, indeed of formalism, in American higher education lasted barely a generation. It was blown to smithereens by the massive student assault on the universities in the late 1960s. But in a provocative book, Allan Bloom would have us believe that the defenses of formal academe were breached not only by the students who poured over its walls but by the faculty who, from the 1940s, tunneled under its structures. Chief among the notions that riddled the forms of undergraduate education were those of moral and cultural relativism. Given impetus in an America experiencing ever broader bands of immigration in the 1940s and 1950s, and worried constantly by foreign wars of ideology, cultural relativism seemed to offer a comforting way to avoid confrontation.

To Bloom, it carried a meaning far deeper and more sinister than that, a meaning born of an antirationalist tradition that descended from Rousseau via Nietzsche to Freud and Max Weber. The relativism Bloom identifies implied an arrant rejection of reason as the basis for truth. Reason to the intellectuals of this generation might yield information and it might provide an invaluable tool for most academic methods, but it could not satisfactorily clear that crucial public ground where all citizens could agree to agree and could get on with the business of the day. Indeed, the very universality of the claims for reason undermined its validity to the relativists. Bound by the German notion articulated at the turn of this century that individual cultures create not only their own satisfactions but their own truths and their own standards of veracity, the relativists scorned any claim to a form that might contain—or even sketch—the whole dignity of man. There was no common ground of experience for them, and, more devastating, there was nothing universal to believe in, except the wrongheadedness of belief itself. With such a network of suspicion girdling the edifice of the liberal arts, it is no wonder that it fell at the first assault.

According to Bloom, there was nothing to replace it. The Weimar Republic that in architecture had given us Mies van der Rohe erected no geometric shapes on the ruins of the American curriculum. Finally, the much vaunted nihilism of the German academy produced just that in America: no directions, not even any signposts to our civilization for the young. They were on their own.

Whether or not Bloom is correct in positing a Germanic *Veltanschaung* to the 1960s, we have been living and teaching for almost a generation now in a world of curricular relativism. Most colleges and universities have installed that relativism, not by some Nietzschean invention of a new academic culture, but by retreat into smaller truths, the truths of various disciplines content to ignore, whenever possible, those of their neighbors. Our own fragmentation has suited the professional ambitions of our students. They have been left largely to pursue their specific interests without larger requirements, which is to say they have studied the skills and techniques by which they hope to earn their living. Rather than a Lever Building, we seem to have erected a series of Habitats made with industrial materials and suitable for the working population. Over the 1970s we provided "used and useful" curricula. We no longer had either a cleared ground for public discourse or a just presentation of human dignity.

And to our considerable credit, we missed them both! Our current debate about the liberal arts is brought on not by any war or even by any student revolution. It is fostered by our reflections upon what we do, what our society does—or does not do—well, and what our most respected predecessors held to be our professional trust. We are not content to abandon the liberal arts, for we know that they are essential to the survival of a free society. Democracy, not to mention democracy in a technological world, requires education beyond specialties. It requires public discourse and the means to arrive at decisions that can be agreed upon. We must have an intellectual clearing in order to operate.

Surprisingly, nowadays, political sharing begins not in the social sciences or the humanities but in the unlikely corridors of mathematics. But the mathematics of our public arena is not the harmony of calculus by which we predict the trajectories of objects in motion and open the gateway to physics. It is, instead, a finite mathematics that supplies paradigms of social science and enables us to evaluate the statistics by which the variety of our political experience is described. It enables us to penetrate the reasoning of bureaucracies, which, by definition, must look for the utility of the greatest number, but which cannot be allowed to chart that utility by their own caprice. Finite mathematics introduces students and then citizens to quantitative reasoning, which enables us to pose problems in algebraic language, to reduce their complexities to discernible entities, and to drive forward to a set of testable solutions.

This reasoning, parallel to the reasoning of technology and, indeed, participating in it, is fundamental to the ways in which major problems are addressed and solved in contemporary society. What is the nature, and what is the impact, of acid rain? Are there feasible inhibitors to its spread? Which of these are cost effective? By what measure of cost? Both statistical sampling and technical analysis are presumed here before a citizen can be genuinely enfranchised to influence decisions. If our students cannot learn to share these skills, we shall have failed to empower them fully to participate in the policy. But if we plan to do so, we must examine radically the expectations and the skills of our mathematics departments. Are we prepared to teach, perhaps even to require the totality of our students to learn, the fundamentals of risk analysis and decision theory, the analysis of gross data and the modeling of statistical hypotheses? Are we requiring high schools to teach the algebraic skills that would enable students to enter such classes? Can we do this?

I would suggest that our debate about the new liberal arts should begin, as the Sloan Foundation would have it, right here. And unless we can persuade the schools to join us in this effort by teaching algebra and geometry squarely in their fundamentals, our new structures will soon collapse.

This is not to say that the old Lowellian "distribution requirement" in natural science, where it still exists, should be supplanted by finite mathematics. There is an intellectual coherence in the demand that students be introduced to both the empiricism of scientific method and the elements of our dominant philosophies, biological and physical; and that coherence is fully sufficient to justify a whole segment of general education. But the reason for such a decision is intellectual and not social, and it will rest always with the proclivities of a given faculty.

Quantitative reasoning, on the other hand, will help us to clear the arena for political discourse. But data analysis alone is unlikely to provide a fully persuasive public conversation. Nor, short of an Orwellian anti-Utopia, should it. For however technical the solution of our problems, their hierarchy will always be determined by human need and by human dignity. And to agree upon these things, we must understand one another—not merely communicate with one another, but *understand*. We must be able to tell our stories and present our interpretations. English language and expression is the second great support of the liberal arts.

Fortunately, we are beginning to move beyond our despair over students' abilities (or lack of them) to write. Work in secondary schools engaged in projects to encourage writing across the curriculum indicates that more of our students can write than we in the universities are accustomed to admit. But they write in the narrative and not in the analytic mode. They tell stories to one another, they are accustomed to hearing stories, and they can use stories to make a point. But they do not easily analyze and they resist the rhetoric of argumentation.

So, too, do our recent immigrants to this country respond first in a narrative mode to the language. Teachers of

English as a second language find that those who are very new to the language are able to recount their months of emigration in terms as searing as any in the nineteenth century.

Entering students in the universities have an English mode of expression which, in widely differing degrees, they do share. They enjoy it, they can play with it, and they can learn by building upon it. We can return Freshman English to a supporting role at the heart of liberal education if we will attune our ears to hear not necessarily their idiom (though perhaps that too), but the capacities of their form of expression. This may mean that we will select from a new range of texts, including Derek Walcott as well as R. K. Narayan, but that range will assuredly deepen the students' own voices as they speak with one another.

For a fundamental goal in all writing courses is to encourage each student to develop his or her own voice. With freshmen we must broaden that goal to include recognition of ways in which voice shapes experience. Narrative, description, analysis: each pattern of speaking is also a pattern of perception. It informs the speaker's life. Students must be helped to recognize their habitual ways with words and to learn that by them they shape their experiences, by them they can identify their habitual patterns of thinking, and by them they can clear their own public arenas of discourse. Just as important, students must recognize the discourse of others and identify the experience that underlies it. If this can occur, we shall have reestablished the ground in this generation for a shared understanding, shared because language will have become once again the means of exchanging experience.

English and mathematics are the twin supports for a new liberal arts intent upon defining the space, the arena, of public understanding. The materials that compose them, indeed their tensile strength as I describe them, may be controversial, but their general priority in the structure will probably be admitted. The real question comes when we debate the cultural foundations of the new curriculum. Should it be, *can* it be, classical and western, employing a dominant integrated motif? Or must it be polymorphous, representing equally the accessible cultures of the world?

Quite simply, I shall argue for a form of classicism; for a general introduction for all students to the history and the texts of this culture, not because they are superior to any others, but because they are particular to this polity. They have informed its past, and they chart its future. Simone Weil has caught our necessity:

> It is useless to turn away from the past to think only of the present. It is a dangerous illusion to even think it would be possible. An opposition between present and past is absurd. The future doesn't bring us anything, doesn't give us anything; it is for us to build it, we must give ourselves to it, even give our lives. But to give, it is necessary to possess, and we possess no other life, no other lymph, than the treasures inherited from the past, as digested, assimilated, recreated by us. Among all the needs of the human soul none is more vital than the past.[8]

Without knowledge of our past we are radically deprived and literally disinherited. It does not matter whether students gain that knowledge from a course (or more) that will present to them great texts, or whether they proceed more chronologically by the contextual study of history. Arguments can be made for either side, and decisions should fall with the skills and interests of the faculty.

For this will be the greatest impediment to reestablishing such a course: many of our faculty, either by the date of their own educations or by their acceptance of cultural relativism, will be quite unwilling to teach the larger texts of our history. In a sense, the first step towards a revised liberal education must be a set of honest and searching faculty seminars. Goals of those seminars and also of any subsequent core courses should not only be modest but they should reflect our negative awareness of the possible pitfalls and biases of the undertaking.[9] Perhaps we can no longer present a narrative of promise or of progress. But we can rejoin ourselves to elements in our own past and understand their context. We can retrace the patterns of our belief and the ongoing conversations about them. And we can hear the music of our own language and know that poetry both sings and persuades.

And if we do these things we shall not impoverish or insult those members of our community who come from another history and another part of the world. In fact, one of the harshest problems we face in our universities and colleges at this moment is the disappointment engendered by our own relativism. It is absolutely true that in the past forty years academic communities in this country have achieved a remarkable pluralism, particularly among students, but even within faculties. Our students are extremely tolerant. But in many cases, theirs is a negative tolerance. We accept persons of any creed or culture because we do not fear that those creeds or cultures, at base, threaten us. We can afford to be neutral, and we are just that, because we are not in jeopardy. But minority students are increasingly finding such neutrality dismissive. It holds nothing to be vital either in the majority or in the minority culture. Deprived of its own significant past, such neutrality denies significance to anyone else. We are all diminished by negative contact.

If, however, we will embrace once again our own history and the body of our texts which have shaped it, we will not only have a respect for our own public ground but we will have a vantage point from which we can learn to see another's. If we will accept once again the classical inheritance of our own tradition, we can also—and we should—require our students to study another culture. The point of such study is not to reenact the indifference that so easily comes of cultural relativism, but to engage the imagination of a student who has learned to recognize who she is, and who can now see the real points of difference which define another. From this vision comes not only tolerance for alien forms, but sympathy for the human heart. In the end, such education might lead not only to knowledge, but to grace.

Notes

1. Charles Jencks, *Language of Post-Modern Architecture* (London: Academy Editions, 1977). See also Paoli Portoghese, *After Modern Architecture* (New York: Rizzoli, 1982).

2. President and Fellows of Harvard College, *General Education in a Free Society* (Cambridge, Massachusetts: Harvard University Printing Office, 1945), Introduction, p. viii.

3. *Ibid.*, p. 44.

4. *Ibid.*, p. 207.

5. *Ibid.*, p. 214.

6. *Ibid.*, p. 224.

7. *Ibid.*, p. 190.

8. Simone Weil, *L'Enracinement* (Paris: Guillinard, 1949). Translated in Paolo Portoghese, *After Modern Architecture* (New York City: Rizzoli, 1982) p. 27.

9. Johnson, "Pasts and Presences in the West" (Curriculum white paper, Mount Holyoke faculty meeting, April 3, 1987).

Defining Our Future

The Liberal Arts in Contemporary Society

RICHARD W. LYMAN

THE WORLD OF PHILANTHROPIC FOUNDATIONS, LIKE other spheres, has its own characteristic rhetoric. Two favorite words in foundationese are "catalyst" and "modest." The supreme ambition of many foundations, to judge from the way they describe their work, is to play the part of a modest catalyst in some process that *other* people are carrying forward.

It is not clear how many foundation officers understand that a catalyst, at work in a chemical reaction, does nothing to alter the nature of the reaction; it merely acts to speed the process by which the reaction takes place (or so my dim recollections of high-school chemistry tell me). I suspect that many program officers would not in fact be satisfied by such a role, to judge from the frequency with which foundations lay down conditions in their grantmaking—We'll give you the money if you'll make the following changes in your proposal or project. In such contexts, use of the word "catalyst" is disingenuous.

So, surely, is the word "modest." All of our grants are modest, or so we say. I can think of at least two reasons for our addiction to this word. Not only is it a defense against

41

excessive expectations—a modest grant can only be expected to produce modest results—but it is a figleaf to cover personality traits more commonly associated with arrogance than with modesty, traits widely thought to be endemic in organized philanthropy.

Having said all this, I now want to put the word "modest" to honest use—painfully honest. Winston Churchill purportedly described his opponent, Clement Attlee, leader of the Labour party, as "a very modest man who has much to be modest about." (He also is said to have called Attlee "a sheep in sheep's clothing.") Poised here to talk about "New Perspectives in Liberal Education," I am forcibly reminded of these gibes and am only grateful that Dean Henley has not introduced me in Churchillian style.

It is, after all, twenty years since I last taught a regular university course, and nearly seven since I left the university world. Furthermore, ours is not a foundation that addresses itself very much to the problems of liberal education. So my place in the distinguished list of lecturers who have been invited to assist this fine institution in celebrating its one hundred twenty-fifth anniversary is clearly that of the outside amateur, no longer a true member of the guild. I shall take what comfort I can from the fact that to look at anything in perspective, one more or less must get outside of it. And also from the fourth definition of "perspective" in the *American Heritage Dictionary:* "the appearance of objects in depth as perceived by normal binocular vision." I offer, then, a "normal binocular" view of the current state of liberal education in the United States. Let us hope it may be, if not especially original, at least modestly catalytic.

"The American college, it would appear, is in crisis again," writes Peter Brooks, who directs the Whitney Humanities Center at Yale:

But it's a strange sort of crisis—not the noisy upheaval of the late 1960's, rather a quiet malaise, a sense that the goals of college have become obscure, its spirit of mission fatigued, its students driven by careerism, its faculty more interested in professional advancement than in teaching, its intellectual core threatened by meltdown.[1]

The Quarterly Review of Doublespeak—the periodical's very existence suggests the presence of some shortcomings in liberal education—tells of a school that announces: "There will be a modified English course for those children who achieve a deficiency in English." It also tells of a Commerce Department employee who asked for a raise and was told: "Because of the fluctuational predisposition of your position's productive capacity as juxtaposed to government standards, it would be monetarily injudicious to advocate an increment." In short, not till you become a steadier performer.

Small wonder that Lewis Lapham, who edits *Harper's Magazine*, derides "entire vocabularies of jargon—literary as well as military and academic—[that] describe kingdoms of nonexistent thought."

An angry letter to the editor of the *New York Times* is headed "College, Unfortunately, Is Nothing but a Product." Another demands: "Is All This Education Necessary?" and goes on to ask:

How did we manage to survive the year 1900, when only 6% of Americans graduated from high school? Why do we have 30 million to 40 million functional illiterates and a citizenry where the average person reads on a sixth-grade level, while 45% are unaware that the Soviet and the United States fought on the same side in World War II, 48% of adults never read a book, and 94% are unable to name their Congressman. . . . Is it comforting to know that our country now has oodles of degrees combined with at least 9 million unemployed and the highest crime rate in the world?[2]

That kind of diatribe can perhaps be dismissed as a case of using education and its shortcomings as what sociologist James March calls "a garbage can issue," into which the antagonist empties every failure, perceived and real, of the society as a whole. But we also have testimony from a well-informed critic centrally placed to observe what is going on—Robert M. Rosenzweig, president of the Association of American Universities, of which this institution and the other major research universities are members:

> In the last year or two I have noticed a disturbing growth in cynicism about universities, the one attitude that I believe we cannot long survive. None of society's institutions, save perhaps organized religion, depends more than universities on the public belief that their purposes are different from those of other organizations—more public-spirited, less self-interested—and the corresponding belief that the conduct of universities will match their purposes.[3]

One could go on quoting more or less severe outbursts of individual criticism ad infinitum. There have been numerous full-scale, systematic critiques as well, some of the most widely heard being *To Reclaim a Legacy* (1984), written by William Bennett when he was still chairing the National Endowment for the Humanities; *Integrity in the College Curriculum* (1985), produced by the Association of American Colleges (AAC) with the aid of a distinguished nineteen-person advisory committee; Ernest L. Boyer's book, *College: The Undergraduate Experience in America* (1987), sponsored by the Carnegie Foundation for the Advancement of Teaching, of which he is president; and a most remarkable volume by Allan Bloom, Professor of Social Thought at the

University of Chicago, provocatively entitled, *The Closing of the American Mind: How Higher Education Has Failed Democracy and Impoverished the Souls of Today's Students* (1987). In addition, the interest shown by many state governors and members of legislatures in reforming the schools has expanded to include studies of the condition of higher education, and the president of the Education Commission of the States, Frank Newman, is making speeches raising such awkward questions as why more than half the students who enter four-year institutions drop out without having earned a baccalaureate degree. When dropping out reaches that level in the high schools it sets off alarm bells, and in fact it seldom reaches such levels except among the most disadvantaged students in the most deprived inner-city schools.

A variety of factors contribute to this widespread and often acute dissatisfaction with the state of higher education. Some of the same worries that have led to concern over the schools contribute to concern over the colleges; in particular, our nation's apparently swift and as yet unchecked downhill slide in ability to hold our own competitively with the rest of the world. It was shocking enough when our balance of trade was seen to be dependent on agriculture, with the competitiveness of our manufactures steadily eroding. Now that we see decline even in our supposed citadel, high technology (the balance is currently favorable thanks only to our aircraft industry), some kind of linkage with our approach to training our population at all levels seems an inevitable public inference.

Add to this such symptoms of inattention to the serious business of higher learning as the campus drug culture, the persistence of the social mores of Animal House, and the seemingly endless series of exposures of scandal and corruption in big-time intercollegiate athletics. It is scarcely surprising that murmurs are heard in the land, or that fresh attention is paid to familiar grievances: too many courses taught by teaching assistants while the faculty sharpen up their grantsmanship; the development of essentially market-driven behaviors at the expense of any coherent educational philosophy; and, perhaps most painful of all, tuition increases in the 1980s which considerably outstrip inflation. Let us, for just a moment, recall the man who declared higher education to be nothing but a product. Nothing provokes questioning of a product's quality like finding its price zooming. Secretary Bennett has drawn real blood, no matter how unfairly, by picturing college and university administrators as feeling able "blithely to raise their tuitions, confident that federal loan subsidies would help cushion the increase."

Beyond the noisy arguments over costs, in which, frankly, few of the participants come off sounding particularly dignified or respectful of the facts in what is a pretty complicated set of circumstances, there lies the growing suspicion that, whatever may be the glories of the American research university at the level of specialized graduate and professional study and scientific inquiry, the colleges have not distinguished themselves of late in their education of undergraduates—which, after all, is what most Americans in the street are thinking of when they think of "college."

What are the headings of the indictment?

First, there is no agreement in higher education as to the overall purpose, no consensus as to what today constitutes an adequate "liberal education." What should the educated citizen in the 1990s have learned in college? As the AAC Report says:

As for what passes as a college curriculum, almost anything goes. We have reached a point at which we are more confident about the length of a college education than its content or purpose. . . . The . . . collapse of structure and control in the course of study has invited the intrusion of programs of ephemeral knowledge developed without concern for the criteria of self-discovery, critical thinking, and exploration of values that were so long central to the baccalaureate years. The curriculum has given way to a marketplace philosophy. . . . Fads and fashions, the demands of popularity and success, enter where wisdom and experience should prevail.[4]

Second, there is no serious effort to determine the "value added" from a college education. The state governors, naturally anxious to know what the voting taxpayers' higher education dollars are buying, are focusing with particular energy on this question. In 1986 the National Governors' Association set up a task force on college quality chaired by Governor John Ashcroft of Missouri. "The job of the panel," Ashcroft reports, "was to determine how much undergraduate students are learning in America's colleges and universities. . . . But we discovered that we couldn't answer the question. . . . Because the majority of our nation's colleges and universities do not have a systematic way to assess how much their undergraduates are learning."[5] And a state senator in Wisconsin lashes out: "We all cluck about having a world-class university, but that's become empty rhetoric. We need to know exactly how we benefit from the dollars we spend."[6]

Third, higher education seems to be still struggling to find the right relationship between undergraduate education and preparation for a vocation. On the one hand, in many institutions that are heavily dependent on tuition the liberal arts are being driven out by programs and courses aimed at assuring the graduate of immediate, short-term success in the job market. But on the other hand, what are the graduate's chances of securing a foothold in the worlds of commerce and technology after emerging from four years at Old Siwash with a major in Art History and a minor in the Metaphysical Poets? Who has found the right balance here? Or must the liberal arts major either take work for which he or she feels overqualified, or go on to graduate school to prepare for the serious business of making a living (and paying back all those loans that Secretary Bennett seems to forget must be repaid)?

Fourth, the academic major reigns supreme, but it means drastically different things, not only from one college to another but from one academic department to another. In the humanities and social sciences, it generally lacks sequencing (and therefore much chance at depth), while in other fields it often stresses content over learning the methods of inquiry. It used to be comfortably assumed that, whatever depths of shallowness might be characteristic of the undergraduates' work in general education, at least there would be intellectual challenge and discipline in the field of concentration. That assumption is now widely questioned.

Fifth, outside the major there tends to be an open cafeteria, with an appallingly large number of dishes from which to choose. The only guidance is rather mechanical and unsubtle, namely, the "distribution requirements" measured in credit hours, a system more likely to conceal than to reveal the underlying logic (if any, beyond logrolling among departments), and often distressingly easy to evade in the spirit if not the letter. Before changes that I spent more than half of my decade in the Stanford presidency working to achieve, I used to observe that it would require quite a concerted and intelligent effort on the part of an undergraduate with anything like the normal curiosity of a twenty-one-year-old to complete the 180 units needed for graduation at Stanford *without* having completed, inadvertently, the distribution requirements.

Sixth, and this is hardly a fresh insight: undergraduate teaching is low on the list of priorities in all but the small liberal arts institutions (even at some of these, the more famous ones, research attainments loom large), and especially so at the research universities that are usually seen as the flagships of the fleet. In fact, more than one professor in four at the research universities teaches no undergraduates whatever. The AAC Report is emphatic on this point:

> Research, not teaching, pays off in enhanced reputation, respect of peers beyond one's own campus, and access to funds. The language of the academy is revealing: professors speak of teaching *loads* and research *opportunities*, never the reverse.[7]

Finally, there is simply a perception that the major universities, as institutions, have become increasingly less distinctive from the rest of society's institutions. As Robert Rosenzweig writes:

> If I had to compress all of the individual signs into one overarching reason for the increase in cynicism, I would say that we are now beginning to see the consequences of the fact that our major universities have become very large and complex institutions, which look remarkably like large and complex businesses. Of course, that is not all they are, but by the measures of asset value, cash flow, size of staff, capital budget, litigation volume, investment activity, and labor relations, universities are indisputably big business.[8]

Nor is the result merely increased difficulty in perceiving the continuing temple of learning in the midst of all this quasi-commercial whirl of activity. When, as happens, universities are seen as pushing at every financial frontier and seizing every available financial opportunity and advantage, even though they remain well within the bounds of ethical behavior, let alone the law, they lose some of that cachet they had in earlier days.

The attempted responses from higher education to all these charges and pointed queries are, of course, various. How could it be otherwise, considering the large number of quite distinct species in the postsecondary educational bestiary? There is some tendency to wax defensive, particularly in the face of Secretary Bennett's almost daily harassments. Defensiveness is seldom a winning strategy, especially when, as in this case, it tends to take the form: "Sure, there's something in what he's saying, but he goes too far—and besides, he's irresponsible and demagogic."

The whole argument over costs and prices is made difficult by the diversity in higher education. To begin with, there is the large difference between the public and private sectors overall. Then there are big differences within each sector, and especially among private institutions. But these cannot be taken at face value, either, since the Harvards and Stanfords offer financial-aid packages that their poorer brethren in the private sector cannot begin to match. So, for any given needy student, going to Harvard or Stanford may be more manageable financially than going to a liberal arts college that has neither endowment nor much in the way of resources to spend on financial aid. One gets the impression, however, that Secretary Bennett is interested neither in addressing such differences nor in really clarifying the issues. He has found a handy way of defending the

Administration's reductions in federal aid, and he no doubt enjoys the confusion in the ranks that his barbs provoke.

On the other side of the equation is the much more interesting matter of what a student can hope to obtain from higher education in America, whatever the price. Here, there is considerable scurrying about, and a mixture of over- and underresponsiveness that is rather familiar. Taken as a whole, higher education has tended to be overresponsive when it comes to proving itself vocationally useful, and underresponsive in relation to anything that seems at all threatening to faculty prerogatives. Thus, anything relating to computers has a headstart in the competition for institutional resources, because computers are vaguely seen as a vital ingredient in everyone's employment success. But the faculty's readiness to explore what the nation's governors may have in mind in their call for more assessment is less than conspicuous.

Proposals for learning to measure, and then measuring, the value added by college naturally arouse fears of national norms and a possible deadening conformity as both states and individual institutions struggle to gain an edge in the ratings and, therefore, to qualify for more dollars in their budgets. Yet what is striking about the governors' plea is its sophistication. As Governor Ashcroft puts it, they "focused not only on the acquisition of knowledge, but also on the improvement of those abilities and skills—such as critical thinking, oral and written communication, problem solving, decision making—which should be part of an undergraduate's experience." Furthermore, he writes:

> assessment should always be tailored to institutional mission, and should take into consideration what kinds of students the institution attracts, the goals of the academic

program, and the knowledge, abilities, and skills that all
undergraduates should develop in their college careers.[9]

It would be hard to dismiss that as a demand for rote learning followed by massively standardized testing.

Deciding what the *desirable* results of four years in college
are, let alone testing for them, presents formidable difficulties. The American tendency is almost always to try to do
too many not-necessarily-compatible things at once. We
want, in the jargon of our time, to "have it all": marketable
skills; the attributes that make up good citizenship; self-
fulfillment along whatever lines the self may select, combined with better coordination of our efforts, and therefore
subordination of self, for purposes of catching up with the
Japanese; strong internalized values that will protect us
from becoming mere money-grubbers, combined with
broad tolerance of the values of other people, cultures,
races, nations, no matter how strongly these are in conflict
with our own. And on and on.

Take just one rather interesting development of the last
few years, the growing concern that, in Benjamin Barber's
words, "the domain of the citizen is vanishing in America."
Ten years ago, a study by the Public Agenda Foundation
entitled "Moral Leadership in Government" found that
"Americans fear that the country has been tending toward
a psychology of self-interest so all-embracing that no room
is left for commitment to national and community interests. . . . They fear that the very meaning of public good
is disappearing, drowned in a sea of self-seeking."[10]

Academia's response has been to develop schemes for
greater involvement of undergraduates in public service of
various kinds. Nothing new here—Phillips Brooks House
has been a center for student volunteering at Harvard for

ninety-three years. But now scores of college and university presidents have formed the Coalition of College Presidents for Civic Responsibility to spread the word, exchange ideas, offer inducements in hopes that students will develop civic consciousness by performing civic functions—the classical American recipe, "learning by doing."

Sometimes the effort extends into the curriculum. Stanford is planning to create a center in Washington, D.C., somewhat on the model of its campuses overseas that have been introducing the sons and daughters of the Golden West to other cultures for something like a quarter-century. At Harvard, Derek Bok has made education for public service as much or more the hallmark of his administration as reviving the Harvard Divinity School was of his predecessor's.

I have much sympathy with all of these efforts; indeed, I preached the inaugural sermon at the first meeting of the Coalition. Yet I also have a nagging feeling that neither facilitation of student volunteer service nor the increase and improvement of professional training for careers in the public sector quite meets the challenge of restoring Thomas Jefferson's ideal of the educated citizenry.

Beneath the superficial revival of national self-confidence, the vision of "America standing tall," and the attempts to conjure up, wildly out of context, John Winthrop's seventeenth century vision of "a city set upon a hill," it seems to me that Jimmy Carter's much-criticized "national malaise" is distressingly alive and well. Buffeted by the chaos in the world and the nightly reiteration of horrible evidences of man's inhumanity to man from Beirut to Belfast and from Sri Lanka to Soweto, frightened by the specter of the Bomb and the present-day realities of drug abuse and Acquired Immune Deficiency Syndrome, we are coming slowly to realize that all those unimaginably big numbers attached to our budget deficits and our appalling imbalance of payments actually do mean something, and that what they mean is we are living far beyond our means. All these phenomena and others are taking their toll, first among the more thoughtful, but eventually even among those who believe the radio news announcers who tell them: "Give us twenty-two minutes and we'll give you the world."

It all adds up to a loss of the sense of moorings, a massive uncertainty as to national goals which cannot indefinitely be obscured on an individual level by careerism and that elusive "self-fulfillment"—uncertainty as to national goals and the destiny of the human race, for no thoughtful person can any longer consider the future wholly in terms of any one nation, not even the most powerful.

The connections should be fairly obvious between our sense of troubles multiplying while solutions recede and our discontent with the workings of liberal education, in what is beyond question the world's most extensive and ambitious enterprise in higher learning. Everyone senses that college ought to be more—infinitely more—than four years of vocational or preprofessional job-readiness training. On the right, there is outcry for more attention to "values," and on the left, alarm at the self-centered and materialistic lives that so many of even the brightest and most promising of our young seem to lead—and to *want* to lead.

We worry about sheer ignorance—the eighth-grade student who thought that Latin is what they speak in Latin America, and that Homer wrote an epic entitled "The Alamo"; the junior at UCLA who thought Toronto was in Italy; the two-thirds of all seventeen-year-olds interviewed in a study by the National Assessment of Educational Progress who did not know that the Civil War took place between 1850 and 1900, and the half who could not identify Stalin or Churchill. In the face of such a mental *tabula rasa*, how do we even communicate with one another, let alone reach an intelligent consensus on questions of national or human purpose? Not long ago I was preparing a commencement address for an East Coast university. I had thought of quoting Oliver Cromwell, but then I realized that in all probability nine out of ten—perhaps nineteen of twenty—in the graduating class would need a potted biography drawn from some one-volume encyclopedia to make the slightest sense of the quotation.

We worry about lack of connectedness. Ernest L. Boyer's recommendation of an "integrated core" (in his book, *College*) speaks to a widely shared feeling that the center has somehow been removed from the collegiate experience. (I am troubled by the widespread use of the word "experience" to denominate what undergraduates are in college to obtain. The word is in Boyer's subtitle; it is on everybody's lips, including, obviously, my own. Yet what it suggests is that education is not a process but a kind of mental—and social and sexual and cultural-cum-aesthetic—hot tub, immersion in which for a few years may prove beneficial, but in ways difficult to specify or express.)

But the "integrated core," while an improvement on what now exists in most institutions, cannot really repair the damage from the late twentieth century's fragmentation. Peter Brooks, reviewing *College* with considerable sympathy, makes the point well:

> The failure of the college curriculum to cohere cannot be attributed simply to failure of nerve or an act of treason by the scholarly caste. The crisis of belief in a core educational experience [that word again!] is authentic, and the task of

restoring coherence is a more difficult and interesting enterprise than Mr. Boyer imagines. His "universalistic"
premise appears as nostalgic as Mr. Bennett's call for a
return to "intellectual authority" as the guiding principle
for a curriculum. Too much of what most matters to us in
modern thought challenges universal premises and sub-
verts claims to authority.[11]

Allan Bloom, in his big, brilliant, erudite, provocative,
sometimes infuriating but impossible-to-ignore book, also
makes the point:

> To repeat, the crisis of liberal education is a reflection of a
> crisis at the peaks of learning, in incoherence and incom-
> patibility among the first principles with which we in-
> terpret the world, an intellectual crisis of the greatest mag-
> nitude, which constitutes the crisis of our civilization.[12]

If what is wrong is "the crisis of our civilization," what
are mere college presidents, deans, and faculty members to
do? Is there any point in trying to design "reforms" to meet
the cosmic, tragic, world-historical need?

I believe that we must try. At the same time, the beginning of wisdom in this matter is to recognize that a higher
synthesis of learning is not likely to be just around the
corner. God may not be dead, *pace* Nietzsche, but St. Thomas Aquinas is, and he cannot be revived by a mandate from
the college president's office or from the secretary of education. Yet there is much that can be improved about this
country's capacity to provide a humane and intellectually
satisfying education for its young.

The first order of business is to try to get the questions
right.

Is the primary question: How do we achieve a common
culture that will bring us together with enough sense of

community to endure the stresses of the contemporary era? I think it is, even though I recognize that one person's fragmentation may be another's cultural pluralism, and that no one wants to be immersed in the notorious "melting pot" again. (I do believe, contrary to much received wisdom, that the melting pot once had and may still have some reality; I remember what it was like to work beside young second-generation Italian-Americans in a New Haven factory forty-five years ago, and to find that most wanted nothing so much as to get rid of the hyphen and be of the new country, not the old.)

Surely E. D. Hirsch, the author of *Cultural Literacy,* is in considerable part right (however one might quarrel with this or that detail of his Appendix, "What Literate Americans Know"): Some shared knowledge base is essential to any society's survival. To expect people to learn to read in a vacuum of information is hopeless; learning to read well involves increasing one's knowledge along the way. One can argue over which of Shakespeare's plays every American seeking literacy should read; it is hard to argue that it doesn't matter whether she or he reads one by Shakespeare or one by Colley Cibber, or, more likely, Neil Simon.

It has been said that students are "preoccupied with the present, apprehensive about the future, and utterly indifferent to the past." That way lies madness—and also despair, the despair of the unrooted. Without more understanding of where we have come from than is possessed by high school (or, often, college) graduates today, there can be no real hope that sensible choices will be made about where to direct our energies or what to cherish in human existence.

What must be supplied is not just any old history. True, the history of any people at any time, studied with enough attention to the evidence (and enough evidence), should increase the students' understanding of how societies change, and therefore of what is and is not possible for human beings living together to accomplish. But we have a particular history, and knowing something of it is surely prerequisite to intelligent participation in this society's agenda. How many college graduates really understand how modern political freedom came into being? How many could explain how it was that we rebelled against British rule because our inheritance of British political thought and institutions made such rebellion inevitable, in the circumstances of the late eighteenth century? Bill Moyers, as thoughtful a person as the television community can turn up, has said: "I worry that my own business [television] . . . helps to make this an anxious age of agitated amnesiacs. . . . We Americans seem to know everything about the last twenty-four hours but very little of the last sixty centuries or the last sixty years."[13] And Christopher Lehman-Haupt has remarked in another context, to live like this "is like being locked in a landscape made up entirely of foreground."[14]

Difficulties abound. For two years at Stanford there has been argument over whether the laboriously revived Western Culture requirement is unfair to blacks, Hispanics, cultures other than western, and women. The argument has been politicized, and—though there appears to be no immediate likelihood of a return to shattering library windows and defenestrating deans as the means of moral suasion—it is impossible not to recognize in the tones of the debate and its *dramatis personae*—the chair of the Black Student Union and the head of the student organization, "Stanford Out of South Africa," have played as prominent a part as the dean of undergraduate studies—the long-range damage done to universities by the anti-intellectual vandalism of the late 1960s.

But I remain encouraged by the persistence of the nation's concern with education at all levels. Given the short attention span of the public on so many issues, I was certain three years ago that education would have slipped from the front of the agenda long before this. Higher education may have hoped to escape, leaving the schools to bear the entire burden. But common sense should tell us that if so much is amiss in the schools, all cannot be well in the colleges. Whence, after all, do the people who teach in and run the schools get their higher education?

It is a good thing that liberal education is once more the subject of active debate. What was dispiriting was to see it pass unmentioned, as it did through the 1970s, or viciously denigrated in the name of liberation from all bourgeois constraints, as it was in the 1960s. Caring about a subject, after all, is the necessary precondition to doing something about it. No doubt we shall never reach calm waters in this turbulent century now drawing to an anxious close. But it is good to know that at least the question of how best to navigate is on a lot of minds again.

Notes

1. Peter Brooks, Review of *College* by Ernest L. Boyer, *New York Times Book Reviews*, March 8, 1987, 22.
2. Letter to *New York Times*, May 5, 1987, 34.
3. Robert M. Rosenzweig, "Seeing Ourselves as Others See Us," *Chronicle of Higher Education*, November 5, 1986, 104.
4. Association of American Colleges, *Integrity in the College Curriculum* (Washington, D.C., 1985), 2.
5. John Ashcroft, "A 'Different' Reform Is Coming," *Higher Education and National Affairs*, December 15, 1986, 7.
6. Senator Mordecai Lee as quoted by Scott Jaschik in "In Wisconsin,

Hard Times and New Governor Prompt Emotional Debate Over College Funds," *Chronicle of Higher Education*, March 11, 1987, 24.

7. AAC, *Integrity in the College Curriculum*, 10.

8. Rosenzweig, "Seeing Ourselves as Others See Us," 104.

9. Ashcroft, "A 'Different' Reform Is Coming," 7.

10. Benjamin R. Barber, "The Real Lesson of 'Amerika'," *New York Times*, May 5, 1987. Public Agenda Foundation, "Moral Leadership in Government," quoted in Meyer Reinhold, "The American Interpretation of Classical Virtue," *Humanities*, vol. 8, January 1, 1987 (published by the National Endowment for the Humanities).

11. Brooks, Review of Boyer's *College*.

12. Allan Bloom, *The Closing of the American Mind: How Higher Education Has Failed Democracy and Impoverished the Souls of Today's Students* (New York: Simon and Schuster, 1987), 346.

13. As quoted by Neil Postman, *Amusing Ourselves to Death* (New York: Viking-Penguin, 1985), 137.

14. Christopher Lehmann-Haupt, "White House Beat," *New York Times*, March 21, 1987, 10 (review of Sam Donaldson's *Hold On, Mr. President*).

One Culture

The True Liberalism

Denys Wilkinson

Some thirty years ago the late C. P. Snow pronounced the Two Cultures: the scientific and the humanistic; he pronounced the Great Divide between them. He was wrong. I want to convince you that he was wrong, or to put it positively rather than negatively, I want to convince you that at the deepest level humankind possesses only a single culture, a single human condition. It may take many forms and may employ many languages—of physics, of politics, of philosophy—but in the end it expresses itself to our consciousness and feeling in the same way whether the starting point is the odes of Horace, Fermat's Last Theorem, the magnetic moment of the electron, a madrigal of John Dowland, or the flight of a curare-tipped arrow. Or, perhaps even more obviously, the first cry of a newborn child. I want, further, to persuade you that in our teaching we must have regard for this essential unity, at the level of which there is no physics, no politics, no philosophy.

All human experience comes to us through the same set of sensory receptors, independent of the context of that experience; those same sensory receptors feed into the same cerebrum, with the same almost unimaginably complex, dendritically linked array of neurons, independent of the context; the firing of the brain cells resulting from those sensory inputs, or from the conscious or unconscious activation of the cells of our memory banks, is the same whether we are dodging a skidding car or contemplating the bust of Homer; we do not have pockets in our brains genetically and exclusively dedicated from birth to physics on the one hand or to history on the other, any more than we have pockets in our stomachs exclusively dedicated to fish or to carrots.

And when it is all over, when the madrigal has died away, when the arrow has struck, what then? If the experience has been run-of-the-mill nothing much happens; our memory banks are marginally readjusted, a few million brain cells change their long-term conditions and interconnections so that the madrigal can be replayed and the fall of the stricken animal revisualized. Perhaps there is then, indeed, a bit of the brain not genetically dedicated but dedicated as a result of such training experiences to madrigals, and perhaps another bit to curare-tipped arrows; humdrum but practical.

But what if the experience has been not run-of-the-mill but exquisitely transcendental? What if Fermat's Last Theorem is suddenly proved? What if the child's first cry strikes such a chord upon our heart strings as never heard before? What if the bend in the road suddenly and unexpectedly presents us with the Grand Canyon glowing unbelievably in the setting sun? What, even this, what if, from the foot of the hero, the ball soars between the posts from a magical distance at a magical moment? What if, whatever it is, it all, after hopeless months or years, suddenly comes out absolutely right? What if, whatever it is, it suddenly could not possibly be other? Such experiences of undifferentiated joy, of incontestable rightness, of identity with some great truth, do not seize our brains or even our hearts; they seize our beings; as Saint Augustine and Oliver Cromwell both put it, they seize our very bowels thereby, incidentally giving the lie to Saint John Chrysostom, who regarded the body as "but the repository of phlegm and spittle." These rare but most precious grand experiences of humankind take us and shake us like the single discharge of some giant synoptic cell; they are epitomes of the purpose of existence; life is nothing without them.

But do these grand experiences have anything specifically to do with mathematics or childbirth or geomorphology or football? Of course not, any more than they have anything to do with the bits of the brain that were responsible for receiving the related sensory inputs or storing the antecedent information. They, in their explosive nature, are the ultimate and literally indescribable expression of the human condition, unique in their nature and mutually identical the one to the other, but capable of being induced, of being loosed off, by myriad unrelated causes.

I oversimplify but I do not exaggerate. These pinnacles of our human experience have a nature and are of an intensity that is unrelated to their primary causes and origins, which might themselves be purely physical, purely intellectual, or purely emotional. It is to these infrequently attained transcendental experiences that we, consciously or unconsciously, attach the greatest value in life, and towards which, therefore, the enabling experiences, again consciously or unconsciously, bend themselves. Consciously or unconsciously, we select our life-styles, within all the socioeconomic and other constraints to which those styles are subject, so as to optimize the chances of our achieving these great orgasmic experiences, these descents, if I might use a semitheological expression, these descents of the divine afflatus.

This emotion of rightness, so sudden and revelatory, so involving of our deepest humanity in its very essence, is sui generis and therefore impossible to describe. Many writers have recognized this. In his Arthur Stanley Eddington Memorial Lecture, Martin Johnson spoke thus of revelatory experience:

> It is also unrecognisable in scientific psychology because externally observable data leave the subjective aspect inaccessible. In that subjective and intimate personal acquaintance we realise that the Good, the Beautiful, the True, imply judgements which we exercise far beyond the guidance of biological instincts of survival, and that beyond those judgements still there is a more shadowy territory. In that territory we discover facts very compelling but difficult to describe adequately. We find the inexhaustible resources of human affection, of self-sacrifice, of persistence of an ideal in loneliness and without hope of reward. . . . Among similar facts are our transfiguration, as in the withdrawal of a mental and spiritual curtain, when, for example, we hear the music of Mozart or contemplate the grace of sea-birds upon mountainous islands. Judicial appraisements, even the aesthetic, dissolve in these experiences, and all judgement is swept away into a surrender of our personality. I think there is no word in the vocabulary to describe our reaction to these occurrences, other than . . . "worship."[1]

This almost literally shattering emotional experience of rightness and its deep and unique relationship with the human spirit were expressed long ago by Plato in the *Phaedrus:* "The soul is awestricken and shudders at the sight of the beautiful, for it feels that something is evoked in it that was not imparted to it from without by the senses, but has

always been already laid down there in the deeply unconscious region."

I have begun at the end and have insisted upon the
uniqueness of this ultimate grand experience of rightness,
of well-being, of joy, of transfiguration, of ecstasy, of revelation: it does not matter what we call it, because it is of itself
and is not to be compared with or related to other experiences or conditions. But we also recognize that there are
stages on the way, not stages on the way to a particular
grand experience, because that arrives out of the blue we
know not how, but in the form of experiences of an essentially lesser order which may nevertheless be of significant
intensity. These lesser experiences we can link in an analyti-
cal way with certain stimuli: a small child dimples and we
say "Oh how sweet!"; we spot a crossword puzzle clue and
we say "Ah ha!"; we suddenly see how to do something, in
the context of it does not matter what, and we say "By Jove!
that's a good idea!" This is not the divine afflatus (when that
descends we most definitely do not say anything: sheer
feeling is of the essence), but it is a kind of significant punc-
tuation mark in the everyday stream of our thoughts and
actions and experiences.

We understand the nature and origin of these lesser experiences; we can relate them to one another and can see that
certain sorts of activity may induce them. And to that degree they are specific to those activities: we have the rock-
ing-the-baby type of experience, the solving-the-differen-
tial-equation type of experience; the getting-out-of-the-
awkward-bunker type of experience; the staying-awake-
until-the-end-of-the-commencement-address (or, as right
now, boring lecture) type of experience; the successful-con-
struing-of-a-tricky-passage-in-Xenophon type of experience. These lesser experiences, in relating specifically to the

type of activity, physical or mental, that gives rise to them, also relate specifically to others of the same class, to others having their origin in the same sort of activity. They eventually become, on the academic or intellectual side, discipline specific; they become related to chemistry or to French literature. As the intensity of the experience falls, they become more and more closely linked to the explicit structure and technicalities of the subsections of our activity from which they spring, more and more dependent upon explicit sideways reference to antecedent similar experiences; they become more and more just the higher points of the pattern of our everyday involvement in our normal tasks.

At this lower level can I, as a physicist, share the delight of the student of the relationships within the verb structures of the Finno-Ugric languages when he perceives a hitherto-unnoticed behavior of the imperfect subjunctive in fourteenth century Estonian verse forms? About as deeply as he can share my delight when I realize that cancellation between terms stemming from heavy meson exchange and isobar excitation permits me to continue to use soft pion theorems even at high momentum transfer.

So at this lowly, although not unimportant, level we have reached the Two Cultures—and Snow is right. But at the level of those supreme grand experiences, the Big Ones, that must arise out of specific activity but are independent of the nature of that activity, we are all only human, experiencing through our common being—and Snow is Wrong. And although you may argue, correctly, that we cannot live on mountaintops, their very existence and accessibility, on rare and glorious occasions, is the reward of life.

Now you may think this all rather high-flown, and again you are right. Than this, nothing could fly higher; that is precisely what I am saying. And, to make a daring foray in the direction of what it is that I am supposed to be talking about (before retreating into the *laager* of my somewhat protracted introduction to it), education has no higher duty than to fit receptive minds to the unity of our human condition, our One Culture, which finds its proof positive in these unifying and transcendental grand experiences.

The second point that I must shout from my mountaintops follows easily and importantly from the first. It responds to the question: "How does human understanding advance?" At any time, within any discipline or activity—and for the moment I shall speak in terms of the conventional academic compartmentalizations—we think we know something. Indeed, we may think that we know a very great deal and may display it in serried tomes and encyclopedias. But truth is, of course, fugitive, as much so in physics as, more evidently, in history. What we call "knowledge" is compounded of "facts," with status ranging from durable verities to downright errors, although at any time we do not know which is which. Plus, at a different and dependent level, it is compounded of structures invented to correlate those facts, permitting extrapolation from them to predict matters that may be susceptible of future revelation by various forms of discovery, accidental or deliberately experimental in the broadest sense. These structures of rationalization, which we invent to correlate the primary data, we call "theories"; if they work sufficiently well over a sufficiently long period of time, we begin to regard them as part of our understanding and to incorporate them into our Weltanschauung. Knowledge, at the factual level, is, of course, valuable but, in my view, somewhat overrated. More important are the correlative theories that, in effect, express factual knowledge in succinct form. But much more important than specific theories is the kind of understanding that, at one level, is a confident synthesis of comfortable theories but that, at a deeper level, is a long-term feeling of rightness; and again I stress "feeling" and relate to the human condition. But, as I have said, truth is fugitive; as Wilhelm von Humboldt recognized as long ago as 1810: "Science is a problem never fully solved and therefore always open." And so, in science as in the arts and the humanities, we must be prepared to lose our precious understanding although not, with it, our reason.

We must recognize that facts are, to some degree at least, facts, although we must neither be blinded by them nor too readily accepting of them, or their relevance, at face value. Remember Ronald Knox speaking through the mouth of the Bishop of Much Wenlock: "Facts are only the steam which obscures the mirror of truth." Remember also Jean-Paul Sartre: "Facts and essences are incommensurables; one who begins his enquiry with facts will never arrive at essence." But, whatever our view of facts, they belong to the world outside us, either objectively, in the sense of being susceptible of repeated verification, as in the case of the helicity of the neutrino, or semiobjectively, in the sense of having been the subject of several independent reports even though the phenomenon was unique and non-reproducible by its nature, as in the case of the Battle of Malplaquet. Nobody will seriously doubt, on the one hand, that the neutrinos emitted in ordinary nuclear beta-decay behave overwhelmingly like left-handed corkscrews, nor, on the other, that Marlborough's defeat of the French in his famous series of battles beginning with Blenheim, Ramillies, and Oudenarde culminated, in 1709, at Malplaquet, that otherwise undistinguished little village in northern France.

But we must also recognize that theories are themselves not objective, or even semiobjective. They are man-made; they are constructs, intellectual artifacts. They are summaries of current currency and current currency only. Thus, the operational left-handedness of the neutrino may be because it is intrinsically and unalterably left-handed, and that is that; or it may be because it is born of the decay of its parent intermediate vector boson, the W-particle, which passes on to its offspring its own left-handedness; but then, is the W-particle itself really left-handed? May there not also exist a right-handed W-particle that is simply somewhat heavier than the left-handed one, so that it does not show up so readily? Is the operational left-handedness of the neutrino, therefore, merely a consequence of the mass relationships between its alternative progenitor particles? Not one theory but a fistful. And thus, also, with the Battle of Malplaquet. Who won it? Marlborough said that he did, but he lost 17,000 men to France's 11,000, which seems a funny way to win a battle, and so it seemed at the time to many back home; perhaps Marlborough simply had the better PR men. And were his great losses at Malplaquet not so much owing to any deficiency in planning or generalship on his part, but rather because his attack was delayed by his allies? Shall we ever know? Will more facts come to light? More Old Kaspars and more skulls, but this time for Malplaquet, not Blenheim? And, indeed, to echo little Peterkin: "But what good came of it at last?" Another fistful of theories.

By definition, all theories work, because that is what they are for, but they cannot all be right. Neither the neutrino nor the Battle of Malplaquet is yet ready for Weltanschauung-incorporation.

In situations such as this, what do we do? In the case of

the neutrino, we carry out all the experiments that are suggested to us by our theories and that are accessible to the facilities at our command. In the case of the Battle of Malplaquet, we resift the archives, restudy contemporary and subsequent accounts, and re-examine everything in the light of developments in military history and in cognate fields, such as psychology, sociology, and politics. But in such cases we are, in the end, for the neutrino as for the Battle of Malplaquet, stuck. We have, by definition, run out of facts and have exhausted the relevant methodologies—scientific, structuralist, whatever they might be. We have nothing to fall back on, no further external points of reference. We have before us just the raw and incomplete facts and the impotent theories. We are on our own; we are left to ourselves. So we mull, we agonize, we mull. The facts rotate and rearrange themselves as we take this point of view and that, as we consciously or unconsciously review everything through the totality of our experience. But facts, like the stars, appear in different constellations to different eyes. Suddenly, the unexpected perception of previously unrecognized relationships between those facts leads to a flash of insight; we are seized in our bowels; it is the descent of the divine afflatus.

That precious flash of insight is not due to the working through of a logical train of thought; it is not due to the pursuit of an established methodology, although doubtless it will be so represented in the subsequent publication. The flash is the same as that grand experience of rightness, the same divine afflatus—unreasoned, unreasoning, and unspecific—that marks any grand experience, irrespective of its origin. The appeal that leads to the descent of the afflatus, for the neutrino as for Marlborough, has not been to physics or to history but to ourselves, to the undifferentiated totality of our experience, when physics and history as conventional disciplines have done their best and have been exhausted; out of ourselves, not out of disciplinary physics or out of disciplinary history, has come the way forward. The flash, the afflatus, is the unspecific expression of our common humanity; we know, with utter conviction, that that way forward is right. Of course, we can be wrong and often are—we are only human.

Indeed, it belongs to the human condition to be human and to err with total conviction, as when Johannes Kepler, after long struggles to understand the number of the planets and their distances from the sun, suddenly discovered that everything could be described in terms of nesting polyhedra. For a moment he had that divine conviction of absolute rightness. But before he went to bed that night he confided to his diary his "horror lest I awake in the morning to find that my joy has disappeared"; in the morning it was, alas, quite clear that it was, indeed, all nonsense.

We can be wrong and often are. In any testing of the human condition we must be prepared to revise our judgments in the light of new evidence or new experience. It may suddenly strike us that behind the shimmering mistiness of the Monet cathedral lies only an architectural drawing, but behind the mistiness of the eyes in the Rembrandt portrait lie the feelings and experiences of a lifetime. And so with the judgments of our deep feelings in relation to science: the course that we chose, perhaps under the slash of Occam's Razor, may in the end turn out to be more tortuous in its subsequent meanderings than the one we rejected at that earlier stage because it then looked more complicated and therefore less attractive; and so we go back and we choose differently. The major judgments in science, as in the rest of life, are always subject to revision as new evidence and experience come along—the "t" of truth is always only a little letter, not a capital. But the judgments, as they are made, are made by Man, and the criteria are always the same, whether those judgments have to do with aesthetics, ethics, or the elementary particles. In the conclusion to his *Critique of Pure Reason,* Immanuel Kant wrote:

> Two things fill the mind with ever-increasing wonder and awe . . . the starry heavens above me and the moral law within me.

I am simply saying that these are not two things but one.

But now I really must turn to my avowed theme of liberal education. I hope that my somewhat self-indulgent setting of the scene has at least prepared you for my thesis, which is that we should educate for an appreciation of the essential unity of our human experience; that we should emphasize in our educational programs the essential humanity of all our studies and activities; that we should, while properly emphasizing the technicalities and the professionalism of the various disciplines or subcultures of academic study, at the same time emphasize the interconnectedness of it all. It constitutes a whole; humankind is not to be sliced up into a multidimensional checkerboard of color, country, race, profession, creed, tongue, except for essentially administrative and bureaucratic purposes, of practical importance, no doubt, but, in the end, trivial. That is what we must teach. How to do it I turn to shortly.

But we must also teach what it is that we do not teach. To know what it is that you cannot know is also an important part of a liberal education. We are not teaching an extreme extension of interdisciplinarity in the conventional sense. We are not teaching that all knowledge and all understanding forms a seamless robe, a proper appreciation of which would enable us to correlate any aspect of the natural world or of human experience with any other, to understand the one in terms of the other by choosing the appropriate route along the surface of the robe between them; and so, ultimately, to know the world as one. That, in my view, is dangerously mechanistic and, indeed, pretentiously nonsensical, arrogating to Man the job of the Gods: "To know is the prerogative of Gods not Men," as Sophocles puts it. No, knowledge and understanding are much more like a patchwork quilt than a seamless robe.

Take an example: From the fundamental laws of physics (of which we are certainly not yet fully aware, but of which we may perhaps sketch plausible caricatures) we construct our account of atoms and of simple molecules; at a rather low level of molecular complexity, the "fundamental" approach of the physicist gives over to the more empirical and pragmatic methods of the chemist with his bond strengths and bail-and-strut models; the chemist in turn passes on the torch to the molecular biologist, thence to the geneticist, to the ethologist, to the psychologist, to the sociologist, to the political scientist, and thence to the psephologist. At each disciplinary interface there is a meeting of methodologies and an authentic and academically respectable sharing of knowledge and tradition. But can we, therefore, on the basis of Coulomb's Law and the Schroedinger Equation, from which the chain starts out at the level of the fundamental physicist, can we say who will be the fortieth president of the United States? But if knowledge and understanding are a seamless robe, why not?

There are many good answers to this question, apart from the kind of contemptuous dismissal that signals an uncertain grasp of the problem. But I will simply emphasize that interdisciplinarity carried to extremes tends to induce the seamless robe syndrome, tends to obscure the patterns of the patchwork quilt, which knowledge and understanding indeed more closely resemble, the contiguous countries of the map of learning. These patterns, although somewhat arbitrary, put rough boundaries around patches of knowledge within each of which questions of a certain type receive answers of a broadly similar nature. And although a thread can be stretched within the surface of the quilt from the patch of physics to the patch of psephology through their linking patches, as I have just enumerated them, and although, as I move along that thread, the language I speak and the things I talk about change in a quasi-continuous way from the one end of the thread to the other, from physics to psephology, that does not mean that it makes the slightest sense to try to resolve the problems of psephology starting from the language of physics, or to aspire in psephology, even in principle, to the quantitativity of physics.

It is worth pausing for a moment to comment on certainty and predictability within physics itself, that most certain of the natural philosophies. It is believed by most, although not by all, physicists that at its deepest level, that of quantum phenomena, Nature displays an inherent and essential unpredictability, with individual events occurring only on a probabilistic basis. But I am not talking about that. Even less am I talking about the outworn notion that this quantum unpredictability may have something to do with free will, and therefore with human behavior. I am talking about a much more relevant form of unpredictability, one which arises in complex systems even when those systems are governed by rigorously deterministic laws such as define classical, as opposed to quantum, physics.

This classical unpredictability now goes by the trade

name of *deterministic chaos;* it has been possible to study it in detail only with the advent of powerful computers, and then only in model form and in relatively simple cases. The point is that if we have a complex, although deterministic, system, such as many ideally elastic billiard balls rattling around forever on an ideal pool table without friction, the observed behavior at any moment, the clashings and paths of the billiard balls, is totally and deterministically specified in terms of the condition of the system at an earlier moment—in principle, at any earlier moment, since from that moment to the one in question, the laws are exact. Indeed, if the two moments are not too far apart, we can easily see how the causal links between them have worked. But as the interval between the moments stretches, we must define the initial conditions at the earlier moment—the previous positions and velocities of the billiard balls—with greater and greater precision in order to predict conditions for the moment of our later observation, because of the increasing number and complexity of the clashings and bouncings of the balls off the cushions. The problem is not the exactness of the laws and the deterministic nature of the behavior, but rather the precision with which we can specify the starting conditions. In fact, as the great computers have shown, the precision with which the initial conditions must be specified to make a meaningful prediction as to the later moment increases explosively with the interval between the initial moment and that later moment in question.

Thus, although the system is totally deterministic, it is impossible to make useful predictions over more than a certain length of time because we cannot, in practice, determine or observe with sufficient accuracy how it all starts off; in principle we can, in practice we cannot, and in the real world it is practice that counts. This, for example, is one factor that limits the reliability of weather forecasting: even assuming that we fully understand, and have correctly parameterized, all the factors that must be fed into the massive computer programs that make the forecasts, the precision with which the input meteorological data must be provided rapidly exceeds the bounds of practical possibility for predictions over more than a very limited period.

So even before we leave physics, the most quantitative and most minutely stitched of the patches of the quilt, we must recognize the practical limits of predictability. And as we progress along our thread from physics towards psephology, the intrinsic complexity of the problems increases, the earlier definition of causality falls away; we must ask different sorts of questions and look for different sorts of answers. And this we must also teach: that seamless robes will be out of fashion for a very long time.

So where does this leave my central thesis, my plea for a new liberal education? I have shown that we cannot look for long threads joining together many patches of my quilt, relating all their essentially disparate methodologies; that does not work; the threads may, at most, tentatively link contiguous patches in pairs. My synoptic image must rather be that the myriad threads, each from its own one of the myriad patches of all knowledge and all understanding, are simply gathered together and tied into one great knot, into which all understanding and feeling flows along those myriad threads. Within that great knot are found those truly common experiences of joy and rightness, those grand experiences that transcend the particular threads along which the knot was reached; and where, when I see the ecstatic fire in the eye of the sociologist, I know that I share his feelings even though I cannot tell one end of a social contract from the other. As Goethe remarked, doubtless with my knot in mind:

Wie alles sich zum Ganzen webt,
Eins in dem andern wirkt und lebt.

which I cannot translate, but which means that Goethe agrees with what I am saying. To explain and transmit these ideas, so great that I hope that you regard them as the merest truisms, would be the truest liberalism. How can we teach this in practice? There is little point in merely waving your arms and making grand assertions as I am now doing. Where might we find the practice of this truest liberalism? Our aim, in educational terms, must be to relate the patches of the quilt—not by linking them through that erstwhile horizontal thread in the surface of the quilt, along which was transmitted, patch to patch, the continuum of academic methodologies, so that one might derive the results of a presidential election from the laws of physics—but rather (to modify my second image) by gathering the individual threads from a few operationally relatable disciplinary patches into a mini-knot. I say "mini-knot" because this is not my grand image of the synoptic knot, where strikes the divine afflatus, but only a small-scale version, although of firmly borrowed imagery. You relate and display the complementarity of the disciplinary patches; you do not try to tie them together permanently in a traditional interdisciplinary way; the knot is tied, and then the knot is untied; you will see how in a moment.

As long ago as 1620 Francis Bacon, in his *Novum Organum*, from his standpoint midway between scholasticism and modern science, had expressed a similar idea:

> But let none expect any great promotion of the sciences . . . unless natural philosophy be drawn out to particular sciences. And again unless these particular sciences be brought back again to natural philosophy. From this defect it is that astronomy, optics, music, many mechanical

arts and, what seems stranger, even moral and civil philosophy and logic, rise but little above their foundation.

What this means operationally for your teaching is that you
choose a topic neither disciplinary nor interdisciplinary in
the conventional sense, but itself complex in its essence, a
topic from the real world, and preferably of some topicality
also; say, for example, "Space." Now Space is not a discipline; you cannot major in it. But it is a significant topic for a
proper overall discussion, and into that mini-knot you
must draw together the threads from quite a large number
of my disciplinary patches: engineering, physics, chemistry, politics, economics, history, geography, and so on.
You uproot your students from their several individual disciplinary patches and put them together around a table, not
with one teacher, that is the whole point, but with a whole
range of teachers together assembled to cover the range of
patches in question—and you talk about Space. As you
talk, each patch makes its own regular disciplinary contribution, and you see how the patches fit together to define
the topic as a whole, each having its essential place. And
you realize that their separate contributions are not different just in terms of facts but also different in modes of
thought; you realize that there are many sets of academic
criteria, each perfectly respectable in its own right, but each
appropriate to its own patch and inappropriate, in varying
degrees, to others; you realize that the living of our life
depends upon not just one but upon many modes of understanding. In this illustration, Space is the little mini-knot
compounded of the many threads, each of which, in making its contribution to the whole, retains its identity and
integrity. Each thread shares its contribution with its fellow
threads; without each thread, the knot could not be tied.

And after you have talked about Space, the knot is untied and the threads return to their parent patches to be recombined in the same or other, perhaps quite different, combinations for other topics, other problems.

Do not mistake me. You were not, in some sense or other, trying to *teach* Space; you were rather using Space as the vehicle for displaying the variety of human thought and for bringing out the sympathy between, and the interdependence of, its components. Such teaching is not easy; it must be tightly structured and guided or it becomes woolly and amorphous; the threads must be kept distinct as their complementary natures are displayed and emphasized. But when properly done it results in a mutuality of trans- (not inter-) disciplinary sympathy and understanding which I am calling the true liberalism. It mixes the sciences and the arts and does not distinguish between them. It also, through this sympathy, leads to a greater sensitivity to the social and human consequences of technological change, and it encourages universities in their great duty of being what has been termed "resources for emancipation." As Alfred North Whitehead put it: "Universities must create the future."

I speak with experience. My own university has, for over twenty years, practiced a mode of teaching, chiefly within the arts, humanities, and social sciences, that is closely related to what I have been describing, although not articulated in the same way. It goes by the trade name of *contextual teaching* and occupies a third to a half of the students' time. To quote from our 1987 Prospectus: "In contextual courses, students from different Majors are brought together in common tutorial and seminar groups, and learn from each other. . . . The system is not intended to produce a graduate qualified in more than one discipline, but to provide a form of education in which, for example, a student in Economics will learn enough about Social Psychology and Politics to be able to use particular insights and analytic methods from those disciplines both during undergraduate studies and in work after university." Examples of such courses now being taught are: "Man and his Image of Nature"; "Imperialism and Nationalism"; "Concepts, Methods, and Values"; "The Modern European Mind." Over fifty such courses are available. We believe, with reason, that such teaching turns out students better fitted for tackling the problems of the real world than does teaching of a purely conventional disciplinary or interdisciplinary kind. This contextual teaching does not have the grandness (I hope "grandioseness" does not spring to mind) of my present vision of the true liberalism, but it at least gives that vision a solid basis in established and successful practice.

I have not spoken at all about pre-university schooling. Nor will I do so except to say that, perhaps paradoxically, I do not believe that my vision begins there at all; it begins only with the bringing together of diverse, firmly established professional and disciplinary bases, such as are acquired by study at university level.

Nor, in all this, must we define the patchwork quilt exclusively in terms of the conventional academic disciplines: we must include everything of relevance to life as it is, in practice, rightly or wrongly, lived. We must have regard for the fact that the human mind is a susceptible and delicate blossom. For example, we must not ignore what I might call the reality of the unreal, the reality of the supernatural, in our promotion of the true liberalism; remember Francis Bacon: "There is a superstition in avoiding superstition." Richard Feynman, speaking in 1964 at celebrations in Pisa marking the fourth centenary of the birth of Galileo Galilei, put it with typical perspicuity and incisiveness. With his mind on any one of our daily newspapers, he imagined Galileo saying: "I noticed that Jupiter was a ball with moons and not a god in the sky. Tell me, what happened to the astrologers?"

Contributors

DR. ROGER SALE is professor of English at the University of Washington where he has taught since 1962, specializing in Renaissance literature. He is the author of numerous books (on Edmund Spenser, modern heroism, regional history, and the writing of essays) and is a regular contributor to the *New York Review of Books*.

DR. ELIZABETH T. KENNAN has been president of Mount Holyoke College since 1978 and president of the Five Colleges Incorporated since 1985. She is a member of the Indo-U.S. Subcommission on Education and Culture and the board of trustees of the University of Notre Dame.

DR. RICHARD W. LYMAN spent most of his academic career at Stanford University serving as its president from 1970 to 1980. He left Stanford to become president of The Rockefeller Foundation, which office he holds to the present.

SIR DENYS WILKINSON served as head of the Department of Nuclear Physics at Oxford University from 1962 to 1976 when he became vice-chancellor and professor of physics at the University of Sussex. He was knighted in 1974.

DR. HERBERT L. COSTNER, volume editor, is professor of sociology and former associate dean of the College of Arts and Sciences at the University of Washington. He served as chair of the faculty committee on the 125th anniversary of the College of Arts and Sciences, which committee organized the series of lectures that form this volume.